Jigsaw

Insightful Reading to Successful Writing

Robert Hickling
Jun Yashima

NATIONAL
GEOGRAPHIC
LEARNING

Australia · Brazil · Mexico · Singapore · United Kingdom · United States

Jigsaw INTRO—Insightful Reading to Successful Writing

Robert Hickling / Jun Yashima

© 2021 Cengage Learning K.K.

Photo Credits:
Cover:© Frans Lanting/National Geographic Creative; 9: ©stock.adobe.com; 10: ©stock.adobe.com; 12: ©stock.adobe.com; 15: ©stock.adobe.com; 16:©stock.adobe.com; 18: ©stock.adobe.com; 21: ©stock.adobe.com; 22: ©stock.adobe.com; 24: ©stock.adobe.com; 27: ©stock.adobe.com; 28: ©stock. adobe.com; 30: ©stock.adobe.com; 33: ©stock.adobe.com; 34: ©dpa/時事通信フォト; 36: ©時事[大塚製薬提供] 39: ©stock.adobe.com; 42: ©Avalon/時事通信フォト; 45: ©Gemenacom | Dreamstime.com; 46: ©stock. adobe.com; 48: ©stock.adobe.com; 51: ©stock.adobe.com; 52: ©stock.adobe.com; 54: ©stock.adobe. com; 57: ©stock.adobe.com; 58: ©stock.adobe.com; 60: ©stock.adobe.com; 63: ©stock.adobe.com; 64: ©stock.adobe.com; 66: ©stock.adobe.com; 69: ©dpa/時事通信フォト; 70: ©時事; 72: ©stock.adobe. com; 75 ©NASA Image Library; 76: ©NASA Image Library; 78: ©NASA Image Library; 81: ©stock. adobe.com; 82: ©stock.adobe.com; 84: ©stock.adobe.com; 87: ©stock.adobe.com; 88: ©stock.adobe. com; 90: ©stock.adobe.com; 93: ©stock.adobe.com; 94: ©stock.adobe.

For permission to use material from this textbook or product, e-mail to **eltjapan@cengage.com**

ISBN: 978-4-86312-386-1

National Geographic Learning | Cengage Learning K.K.
No. 2 Funato Building 5th Floor
1-11-11 Kudankita, Chiyoda-ku
Tokyo 102-0073
Japan

Tel: 03-3511-4392
Fax: 03-3511-4391

はしがき

　本書 Jigsaw INTRO は、英語を媒介として情報や考えなどを的確に理解したり、適切に伝えたりできるようになることを目的に作られた、リーディングとライティングの統合型テキスト Jigsaw の初級編にあたります。

　Jigsaw との違いは、本書がより基礎的な文法事項やライティング技術の学習に重点を置いている点にあります。とりわけ、各リーディングパッセージを 100 ～ 150 語程度の英文で書かれた読みやすいものにし、文法事項、重要表現、パラグラフ展開が基礎レベルから着実に学べるように工夫してあります。また、ライティングに関しては、一つ一つの英文を正確に書く練習から、考えをまとめてパラグラフを書く練習へと無理なく進むことができるように、ユニークな練習問題を多数用意しました。

　英語の文章には、情報伝達の目的や意図に応じた典型的な構成パターンがあります。本書は、そうしたパターンに従って書かれたリーディングパッセージから重要表現やパラグラフ展開を学び、最終的に学習者自身が情報発信の目的や意図に応じて英語で文章を書けるように、リーディングで学んだことをライティングで実践しながら身につける構成になっています。

　各 UNIT は、個々の英文を正確に読む・書くための文法事項の確認、文と文の論理的なつながりを考える練習、考えをまとめて一つのパラグラフを書く練習から構成されています。最初にリーディングパッセージを読み、そこから文法事項・重要表現・パラグラフ構成を学び、学んだことを使って実際にセンテンスからパラグラフまで段階的に書いてみることによって、読解力と表現力を効率よく磨けるように工夫してあります。

　このテキストを通じて、学習者が自信を持って英語で情報や意見を交換し、積極的にコミュニケーションを図れるようになることを願っております。

著者一同

Table of Contents

はしがき……………………………………………………………………………………… 3

本書の構成と使い方………………………………………………………………………… 6

音声ファイルの利用方法…………………………………………………………………… 8

Unit	Title	Writing Purpose	Grammar Points
1	These Are the Facts	Writing to Inform	現在時制と現在進行形
2	Separating into Groups	Writing to Classify	動詞の種類
3	If I Were You…	Writing to Advise	可算名詞と不可算名詞
4	Sizing Things Up	Writing to Evaluate	人称代名詞
5	Mission Accomplished	Describing an Achievement	過去時制と過去進行形
6	This Really Happened	Reporting an Event	時や場所を表す前置詞
7	Every Problem Has a Solution	Solving a Problem	助動詞
8	Let Me Make It Clear	Writing to Clarify	疑問代名詞と疑問副詞
9	Don't You See It My Way?	Persuasive Writing	to 不定詞・動名詞を目的語にとる動詞
10	One Thing Leads to Another	Cause & Effect	現在完了
11	This Is the Same, but That's Not	Compare & Contrast	比較級と最上級
12	What Do You Think?	Expressing an Opinion	be going to と will
13	Weighing Strengths and Weaknesses	Pros & Cons	従位接続詞
14	One Step at a Time	Describing a Process	受動態
15	Data Presentation the Simple Way	Explaining Graphs	関係代名詞

付録 ·· 99

	Reading Topic	Writing Strategy	Page
Reading 1	Penguins and Polar Bears	事実と意見を区別する	9
Reading 2	Polar Opposites		
Reading 1	Sleep Really Matters	分類に役立つ表現	15
Reading 2	The Four Stages of Sleep		
Reading 1	Job Hunting	提案や助言を表す	21
Reading 2	Transitioning into Your First Full-Time Job		
Reading 1	Reading Books Is Important	文章内の指示と主題の明示	27
Reading 2	Printed Books Versus E-books		
Reading 1	A Product with a Bright Future	同じ表現の重複を避ける	33
Reading 2	A Great "Solution"		
Reading 1	The Birth of Commercial Aviation	直接話法と間接話法	39
Reading 2	Miracle on the Hudson		
Reading 1	Is the Elevator Ever Going to Come?	無生物主語	45
Reading 2	Please Wait		
Reading 1	U.S. Presidents: FAQs	部分否定と言い換え	51
Reading 2	How to Become President of the USA		
Reading 1	Japanese Eating Habits over the Years	情報を追加する	57
Reading 2	Fast Food—A Lifesaver or a Life Breaker?		
Reading 1	Social Media	原因・理由と結果を表す	63
Reading 2	Benefits of Social Media for University Students		
Reading 1	How Halloween Took Off in Japan	トピックセンテンス	69
Reading 2	Halloween in the United States and Japan		
Reading 1	Space Tourism	支持文と結語文	75
Reading 2	The Necessity of Space Exploration		
Reading 1	Telework	対比や対照を表す	81
Reading 2	Is Telework Good or Bad for Workers and Their Companies?		
Reading 1	Buying Shortcuts	出来事の前後関係を表す	87
Reading 2	How Buying Decisions Are Made		
Reading 1	Graphs	数値の動向を表す	93
Reading 2	Graph Talk		

本書の構成と使い方

各 Unit は 6 ページ構成です。以下に、それぞれの項目やアクティビティの目的と使い方を説明します。

Writing Purpose

その Unit で学習する文章のパターンが提示されています。

それぞれの Unit で、特定のライティングの目的にそって書かれた文章を読み、最終的には同じパターンのパラグラフが書けるようになることを目指します。

Warm-Up Questions

Reading 1、**2** のトピックに関する質問に答える問題です。英文を読む前に、トピックに対する問題意識を高めます。

Reading 1

100 語程度で書かれた英文を読み、その Unit で扱うトピックについての背景知識を深めます。音声を聞いて、より深い内容理解をめざします。

Comprehension Questions

本文の内容理解を確認する 3 択問題です。本文の重要ポイントの理解を深めます。

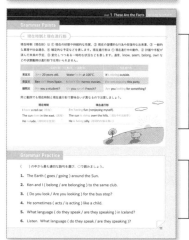

Grammar Points

英語を読んだり、書いたりする上で重要な文法項目を取り上げ、図表などを使いわかりやすく、簡潔に解説しています。

Grammar Practice

Grammar Points で学習した文法項目が身についているかを、2 択問題で確認します。

Reading 2

各 Unit の **Writing Purpose** にそって書かれた約 150 語の英文を **Writing Purpose** を意識しながら読みます。音声  を聞いて、より深い内容理解をめざします。

Comprehension Questions

本文の内容理解を確認する英問英答形式の 3 択問題です。本文の重要ポイントの理解を深めます。

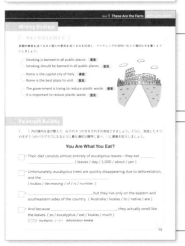

Writing Strategy

英語で文章を書く際に、理解して、使えるようになってほしい表現方法を、例文をあげて解説しています。その Unit の **Reading** で、よく使われている項目が取り上げられていますので、本文でどのように使われているか、振り返ってみることが大切です。

Paragraph Building

各 Unit の **Writing Purpose** に沿ったパラグラフを書くための準備練習です。センテンスの一部が語句の整序問題になっていますので、それを完成してから、センテンスを<u>並び替えて</u>パラグラフを完成します。

Paragraph Writing

A、B または、A、B、C と段階的に各 Unit の **Writing Purpose** にそったパラグラフを書くための練習をします。段階を踏んだ練習をすることで、無理なくパラグラフを書く練習ができます。

音声ファイルの利用方法

 のアイコンがある箇所の音声ファイルにアクセスできます。

https://ngljapan.com/jgs-intro-audio/

① 上記の URL にアクセス、または QR コードをスマートフォンなどのリーダーでスキャン

② 表示されるファイル名をクリックして音声ファイルをダウンロードまたは再生

These Are the Facts

北極と南極は地球上の極地と呼ばれる地域です。写真や映像でしか見たことのない世界なので、漠然と
したイメージしか湧かないという人も多いでしょう。二つの極地は似たような特徴を持つと思われがち
ですが、実際には違いがたくさんあります。この Unit では、北極と南極の特徴について説明した文章
を読み、英語で事実を正確に伝えるための練習をしましょう。

Warm-Up Questions

下の世界地図に示された **1 ～ 7** の大陸の名前をそれぞれ英語で答えましょう。

1. N _ _ _ _ _ A _ _ _ _ _ _ _

2. S _ _ _ _ _ A _ _ _ _ _ _ _

3. E _ _ _ _ _ _

4. A _ _ _ _

5. A _ _ _ _ _ _

6. A _ _ _ _ _ _ _ _ _

7. A _ _ _ _ _ _ _ _ _ _

02
Audio

Penguins and Polar Bears

We often see penguins and polar bears together in advertisements, especially during the cold winter months. In one famous Coca-Cola television commercial, a colony of penguins is

having a Christmas party at the bottom of a hill. A 5▶ curious polar bear cub is watching below, but slips down the hill and lands in front of the surprised penguins. A young penguin then appears and gives the cub a bottle of Coca-Cola. The cub takes a sip and smiles, and the bear family joins the party. It's a great 10▶ commercial. But it's something you'll never actually see for one simple reason—polar bears live in the Arctic, penguins live in the Antarctic.

Notes colony 集団   polar bear cub シロクマ（ホッキョクグマ）の子供   take a sip 一口飲む   Arctic 北極（地方）
Antarctic 南極（地方）

Comprehension Questions

本文の内容に合うように、（   ）の中から適切な語句を選びましょう。

1. In the commercial, the penguins are partying (a. on a mountain   b. at the bottom of a hill   c. on a beach).

2. The young penguin gives the bear cub a (a. bottle   b. can   c. glass) of Coca-Cola.

3. We learn that (a. penguins live in both the Arctic and the Antarctic   b. polar bears live in the Antarctic   c. penguins don't live in the Arctic).

Grammar Points

現在時制と現在進行形

現在時制（現在形）は ① 現在の状態や持続的な性質、② 現在の習慣的な行為や反復的な出来事、③ 一般的な真理や社会通念、④ 公的に確定している予定などを表します。現在進行形は ① 現在進行中の動作、② 計画や手配が済んだ未来の予定、③ 変化しつつある一時的な状況などを表します。通常、know, seem, belong, own などの状態動詞は進行形では用いられません。

	現在時制（be 動詞・一般動詞）		現在進行形
肯定文	I am 20 years old.	Water boils at 100°C.	It's raining outside.
否定文	Ben isn't from Spain.	I don't like horror movies.	I'm not enjoying this party.
疑問文	Are you a student?	Do you speak French?	Are you looking for something?

同じ動詞でも現在時制と現在進行形で意味合いが異なるので注意しましょう。

現在時制	現在進行形
I have a red car. (所有)	I'm having fun (=enjoying myself).
The sun rises in the east. (真理)	The sun is rising over the hills. (進行中の出来事)
He is rude. (持続的な性質)	He is being silly. (意図的な振る舞い)

Grammar Practice

(　　) の中から最も適切な語句を選び、〇で囲みましょう。

1. The Earth (goes / going) around the Sun.

2. Ken and I (belong / are belonging) to the same club.

3. (Do you look / Are you looking) for the bus stop?

4. He sometimes (acts / is acting) like a child.

5. What language (do they speak / are they speaking) in Iceland?

6. Listen. What language (do they speak / are they speaking)?

11

03
Audio

Polar Opposites

1   The Earth has two polar regions—the Arctic at the top and the Antarctic at the bottom. The Arctic region includes the Arctic Ocean, and parts of Canada, Russia, the United States, Denmark (Greenland), Norway, Finland, Sweden and Iceland. The continent of Antarctica makes up most of the Antarctic region. To put it another way, 5▸ the Arctic is an ocean completely surrounded by land, while the Antarctic is land completely surrounded by ocean.

2   Today, about four million people are living in the Arctic, mostly in towns and cities. The city of Murmansk, Russia is the Arctic's largest city, with a population of over 300,000. Antarctica is the only continent on Earth without a permanent human 10▸ population. However, between 1,000 and 4,000 researchers and staff are working on about 70 bases at any given time.

3   Auroras occur in both polar regions—northern lights, or aurora borealis, in the Arctic, and southern lights, or aurora australis, in the Antarctic.

Notes   continent 大陸　permanent 永続的な　at any given time いつでも

Comprehension Questions

本文の内容に関して、次の質問の答えとして適切なものを選びましょう。

1. Which is true about the Arctic region?

  a. It is surrounded by land.   b. It has ocean all around it.   c. It belongs to Russia.

2. About how many people live in the Arctic?

  a. 4,000   b. 300,000   c. 4,000,000

3. What is another name for the northern lights?

  a. artic aurora   b. aurora borealis   c. aurora australis

Writing Strategy

事実と意見を区別する

客観的事実を述べる文と個人の意見を述べる文を区別し、ライティングの目的に応じて適切な文を書くようにしましょう。

- Smoking is banned in all public places. 事実
- Smoking should be banned in all public places. 意見

- Rome is the capital city of Italy. 事実
- Rome is the best place to visit. 意見

- The government is trying to reduce plastic waste. 事実
- It is important to reduce plastic waste. 意見

Paragraph Building

(　　　) 内の語句を並び替えて、以下の 4 つの文をそれぞれ完成させましょう。さらに、完成した 4 つの文が 1 つのパラグラフになるように最も適切な順序に並べ、□ に順番を記入しましょう。

You Are What You Eat?

□ • Their diet consists almost entirely of eucalyptus leaves—they eat _____ _____. (leaves / day / 1,000 / about / per)

□ • Unfortunately, eucalyptus trees are quickly disappearing due to deforestation, and the _____.
(koalas / decreasing / of / is / number)

□ • _____, but they live only on the eastern and southeastern sides of the country. (Australia / koalas / to / native / are)

□ • And because _____, they actually smell like the leaves. (so / eucalyptus / eat / koalas / much)

Notes eucalyptus ユーカリ　deforestation 森林破壊

13

Paragraph Writing

A 以下の表は Sandra Brown という人物の略歴を表したものです。これを参考にして、あなた自身について表の右側に記入してみましょう。

Name	Sandra Brown	
Age	21	
Place of Birth	Chicago, Illinois	
Family	mother, father, younger brother	
Character	hardworking, serious	
Hobbies and Interests	oil painting, reading	
Name and Location of University, Year, Major	Branwick University, New York, 3rd year, art major	
Goal after Graduating	Work as an artist	

B A の表をもとに、Sandra Brown の紹介文を完成させましょう。

Sandra Brown is [1](   ) years old. She's from Chicago, [2](   ).
There are [3](   ) people in her family—her mother, father,
[4](   ) brother and her. She is hardworking and [5](   ). In her
free time, she enjoys [6](   ) painting and [7](   ). Sandra is a
third-year student at Branwick University in [8](   ). Her major is
[9](   ). After graduating, she hopes to become an [10](   ).

C A で記入した内容にしたがって、あなた自身の自己紹介文を書いてみましょう。

Please allow me to introduce myself. My name is _____. I'm from
_____. There are _____ people in my family—_____
_____. In my free time,
_____. I'm a _____
student at _____. My major _____
After graduating, _____.

2

Separating into Groups

みなさんは毎日何時間睡眠をとっていますか。世代別では 20 代前半がもっとも就寝時刻が遅いという報告があります。多くの大学生がついつい夜更かししてしまいがちですが、睡眠は私たちにとって必要不可欠な「活動」であり、決して無意味な時間ではありません。この Unit では、睡眠のサイクルについての文章を読み、英語で分類を表すための方法を学びましょう。

Warm-Up Questions

次の質問に対して該当する答えを選び、☑をつけましょう。

1. How many hours do you usually sleep each night?

   ☐ less than 6 hours   ☐ 6–8 hours   ☐more than 8 hours

2. Do you usually go to bed at the same time every day?   ☐Yes ☐No

3. Do you sometimes have trouble falling asleep at night?   ☐Yes ☐No

4. Is it difficult for you to get up in the morning?   ☐Yes ☐No

5. Do you usually remember your dreams in the morning?   ☐Yes ☐No

04
Audio

Sleep Really Matters

Do you have trouble getting up in the morning? Are you tired during the day? If so, then you're probably not getting
5▶ enough sleep. Doctors say that university students need about 7 to 9 hours of sleep per night. Most students sleep between 6 and 6.9 hours. Sleep is important for a number of reasons. It restores our energy,
10▶ makes us think more clearly and puts us in a more positive mood. It's false to think that sleep is a passive activity. It's a very important active process that's necessary for our physical and mental health.

Notes passive 受動的な　process 過程

Comprehension Questions

本文の内容に合うように、（　　　）の中から適切な語句を選びましょう。

1. Most students sleep about (a. 5 or 6　b. 6 or 7　c. 7 to 9) hours a night.

2. Most students (a. sleep enough　b. don't sleep enough　c. sleep too much).

3. Sleep is an important (a. active　b. passive　c. inactive) process that people need for their physical and mental health.

Grammar Points

目的語をとらない動詞を自動詞、目的語をとる動詞を他動詞といいます。さらに自動詞・他動詞の中には、それぞれ補語をとるものととらないものがあります。自動詞の補語は主語を説明し、他動詞の補語は目的語を説明する働きをします。自動詞と誤りやすい他動詞（discuss, marry, reach, resemble など）には注意しましょう。

	動詞の区別	例文			
自動詞	補語（C）をとらないもの (sleep, swim, walk, laugh など)	The boy (S)	laughed. (V)		
	補語（C）をとるもの (be, become, seem, look など)	Hiroshi (S)	is (V)	a student. (C)	
他動詞	目的語（O）を1つとるもの (have, like, drink, marry など)	She (S)	likes (V)	movies. (O)	
	目的語（O）を2つとるもの (give, show, tell, send など)	He (S)	gave (V)	her (O)	a ring. (O)
	目的語（O）と補語（C）をとるもの (make, call, consider など)	The news (S)	made (V)	them (O)	happy. (C)

Grammar Practice

（　　　）の中から最も適切な語句を選び、◯で囲みましょう。

1. The sun (rises / raises) in the east.

2. This beer tastes (bad / badly).

3. Kate (married / married with) her boss.

4. Tom (explained / told) me the story.

5. He (said / called) me a liar.

6. We're going to (talk / discuss) about the project tomorrow.

05
Audio

The Four Stages of Sleep

1   You may not know it, but a lot happens when you sleep. In fact, there are four main stages in the sleep cycle. Stages 1, 2 and 3 are non-REM (rapid eye movement) sleep, and stage 4 is REM sleep. A complete cycle takes about 100 minutes.

2   The first stage is a period of light sleep. Your muscles aren't totally relaxed yet, and your eyes move a little and may be slightly open. Your body functions slow down. In the second stage, your brain activity decreases in order to enter a deep period of sleep. In the third stage of the sleep process, your brain starts making slow brain waves (delta waves), and there isn't much eye or muscle activity. Your body is busy "fixing" itself and building up energy for the next day.

3   The final stage is REM sleep. This is when most dreaming occurs and your eyes move around in different directions. During this time, your brain stores information from the day before into your long-term memory.

Notes   REM (rapid eye movement) レム（急速眼球運動）   body function 身体機能   delta wave デルタ波

Comprehension Questions

本文の内容に関して、次の質問の答えとして適切なものを選びましょう。

1. What happens during the first sleep cycle?

　　a. Body functions slow down.　b. Eye movement stops.　c. Your mouth opens.

2. What happens during Stage 2?

　　a. The brain becomes more active.　b. Brain activity slows down.
　　c. The brain starts making delta waves.

3. What occurs during the REM stage?

　　a. energy build-up and dreaming　b. rapid eye movement and body repair
　　c. dreaming and moving information into long-term memory

Writing Strategy

分類に役立つ表現

(1) 対象を順序立てて分類する
< first, second, third, next, last など >

- This essay has five paragraphs. The first paragraph introduces the topic. The next three paragraphs make up the body of the essay. The final paragraph concludes the essay.

(2) 対象を特徴や性質ごとに分類する
< one, another, some, others, the other(s) など >

- There are two computers in the room.
  One is mine, and the other is my brother's.
- Some people like him, but others don't.

Paragraph Building

(　　　) 内の語句を並び替えて、以下の4つの文をそれぞれ完成させましょう。さらに、完成した4つの文が1つのパラグラフになるように最も適切な順序に並べ、□に順番を記入しましょう。

Meat, Poultry and Fish

- [ ] _____ of flesh foods. For most of us, it's the only wild food we eat. (the / fish / is / category / third)

- [ ] Meat includes _____, such as beef, pork and lamb. (animals / meats / all / from / red)

- [ ] We generally _____: meat, poultry and fish. (three / flesh foods / divide / into / categories)   Notes flesh food 肉食品

- [ ] Poultry _____ from birds, like chicken and turkey. (food / is / we / the / get)

19

A 以下の語句の表す内容が下の表のどのカテゴリーに分類されるかを考え、それぞれ該当するカテゴリーの下に記入しましょう。

~~autumn leaf viewing~~ / bamboo shoots / going to the beach / cherry blossom viewing / chestnuts / cold / cool / dry / festivals / fireworks shows / hiking / hot / hot spring bathing / humid / illuminations / *mikan* oranges / *nabe* hot pot / persimmons / rainy season / *sakura mochi* rice cakes / shaved ice / skiing / snowboarding / snow / typhoons / warm / watermelon / wearing yukata

Weather	Events & Activities	Food
	autumn leaf viewing	

B A の表とあなた自身の考えをもとに、(1) 日本の四季の各季節の気候、(2) それぞれの季節で楽しみにしている行事や活動、(3) その季節に食べたい（飲みたい）ものを 2 つずつ書き、以下のパラグラフを完成させましょう。

Like many countries, Japan has four seasons: spring, summer, fall and winter. In spring, the weather starts to warm up. I look forward to _____ _____, and eating _____ and _____. It's _____ in summer. I like to _____, and eat _____ and _____ during this season. In fall, _____ _____. The weather is _____ in winter. _____ _____

3

If I Were You…

日本の大学生の多くは、大学在学中に就職活動をして、卒業後すぐに就職します。ほとんどの学生にとって就職は人生で初めての経験です。就職活動とはどのようなものなのか、就職する前に何を準備しておいた方がよいのか、といった疑問や不安を抱えている学生は決して少なくありません。この Unit では、就職に関連する文章を読み、英語で提案や助言を表現する方法を学びましょう。

Warm-Up Questions

次の質問に対してそれぞれ英語で答えましょう。

1. What are three things you like about being a student?

_____ / _____ / _____

2. What are three things you don't like about being a student?

_____ / _____ / _____

3. What are three "dream jobs" for you?

_____ / _____ / _____

06
Audio

Job Hunting

Most university students enter a company soon after graduating. In Japan, job hunting usually starts in the
5▶ students' junior (third) year. During this period, students learn about companies in a number of different ways. This includes attending information sessions, seminars and alumni visits, as well as doing internships and Internet research. Students must also find time to write their résumé, fill out job applications and prepare for job interviews. The job search can sometimes be a quick and easy process. But in most cases, it's a
10▶ very busy and stressful time that takes months of hard work.

Notes alumni 卒業生、同窓生 résumé 履歴書 application 応募（書類） interview 面接

Comprehension Questions

本文の内容に合うように、（　　）の中から適切な語句を選びましょう。

1. A junior is a (a. first-year b. second-year c. third-year) university student.

2. An important part of job hunting is (a. information gathering b. class discussions c. report writing).

3. The job search is usually a (a. simple b. worry-free c. challenging) process.

Grammar Points

可算名詞と不可算名詞

英語には可算名詞と不可算名詞の区別があります。可算名詞の単数形、複数形、不可算名詞は、それぞれ一緒に用いることができる要素が異なるので注意しましょう。

名詞の前の要素	可算名詞（単数）	可算名詞（複数）
冠詞	{a/the} dog	{—/the} dogs
所有格	{my/his/your/John's} box	{my/his/your/John's} boxes
指示代名詞	{this/that} knife	{these/those} knives
数詞	one baby	{two/a hundred/hundreds of} babies
数量詞	{each/every/no} child	{all/a lot of/some/many/a few/few/no} children

※不特定の対象を表す場合、単数名詞には a/an がつき、複数名詞の場合は無冠詞となります。

名詞の前の要素	不可算名詞
冠詞	{—/the} water
所有格	{my/his/your/John's} baggage
指示代名詞	{this/that} information
数詞	——
数量詞	{all/a lot of/some/much/a little/little/no} knowledge

※不特定の対象を表す場合、つねに無冠詞となります。量を表す場合は、a piece of advice
や two cups of coffee のように、単位を示す語句を名詞の前に置きます。

Grammar Practice

（　　）の中から最も適切な語句を選び、○で囲みましょう。

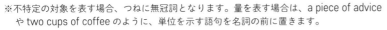

1. They gave me some (advice / advices) on job hunting.

2. I have a few (money / coins) in my pocket.

3. Nancy saw several cute (dog / dogs) in the park.

4. David spends (too much time / too many times) playing video games.

5. One of my (friend / friends) is a famous singer.

6. (Every / All) students took the same test.

07 Audio

Transitioning into Your First Full-Time Job

1   Graduating from university and starting a full-time job isn't an easy thing to do. Following these few pieces of advice, however, may make the transition into the working world a little easier.

2   First, if waking up early is a major challenge for you, then I recommend that you
5▸ start getting up at the necessary time a week or two before your new job starts. This will give your body time to adjust.

3   Second, since you'll be spending a large amount of time with your boss and co-workers, it's a good idea to start talking and connecting with them from day one. Having a great relationship with your new office mates will make going to work each
10▸ day less stressful and more enjoyable.

4   Finally, avoid a "work, sleep, repeat" routine. Life isn't only about work. I suggest that you make time for yourself to meet friends, enjoy a hobby or simply relax at home.

Notes   transition 移行（する）   connect (with someone) （〜と）親しくなる   avoid 避ける

Comprehension Questions

本文の内容に関して、次の質問の答えとして適切なものを選びましょう。

1. What is the suggestion for people who have difficulty waking up in the morning?

   a. go to bed early   b. set several alarm clocks
   c. practice getting up at the right time for at least a week

2. When is a good time to start connecting with co-workers?

   a. on your first day   b. a few days after starting work   c. at your welcome party

3. What does "work, sleep, repeat" mean?

   a. Work is fun.   b. Life is only about work.   c. Personal time is important.

Writing Strategy

提案や助言を表す

(1) 提案者・助言者を主語にした表現

< I recommend..., they suggest...など >

- He suggested that the meeting be postponed until tomorrow.
   ※提案や要求を表す動詞に続く that 節の中では、仮定法現在を用いることに注意。

(2) 提案・助言の相手を主語にした表現

< she should..., you are advised to...など >

- You should make travel arrangements as soon as possible.

(3) 提案・助言内容を（真）主語にした表現

< it's a good idea to..., it's advisable to...など >

- It's a good idea to do some research before shopping online.

Paragraph Building

（　　）内の語句を並び替えて、以下の 4 つの文をそれぞれ完成させましょう。さらに、完成した 4 つ
の文が 1 つのパラグラフになるように最も適切な順序に並べ、□に順番を記入しましょう。

Advice from a Father to His Son

□ • _____ to a son was by Will Smith in the movie
The Pursuit of Happyness. He starts off by saying, "Don't let someone tell you
that you can't do something. Not even me." (the / think / I / advice / best)

□ • The third thing he says is, "When _____
_____, they're gonna tell you that you can't do it."
(can't / people / themselves / do / something)

□ • He concludes by saying, "You _____. Period."
(go / it / want / something, / get)

□ • He then goes on to say, "_____ gotta protect it."
(you / you / a / got / dream,)

   Notes   *The Pursuit of Happyness* 『幸せのちから』（2006 年のアメリカ映画。Happyness のスペルは原題通り）
   (be) gonna = (be) going to ～するだろう　you gotta = you've got to ～しなければいけない

A 下の 1 ～ 3 の悩みに対する適切な助言をそれぞれ (a) ～ (c) から選び、空欄に記入しましょう。

1. "I want to go to Italy this summer, but I don't have enough money. I have a part-time job, but I always spend my money on clothes and entertainment." ☐

2. "I don't have much energy these days and it's hard to get up in the morning." ☐

3. "My friend gets angry at me if I don't reply to her text messages right away." ☐

   a. You should tell her that you're busy and can't check your phone very often.

   b. Why don't you promise yourself to save half the money that you earn?

   c. I advise you to eat healthier food and go to bed earlier.

B 以下は Joe の悩みです。囲みの中の語句を使って、Joe への助言を完成させましょう。

"I'm very forgetful. I often forget to bring my train pass, my wallet and my smartphone when I leave the house, and I sometimes forget important appointments." – Joe –

I also strongly recommend one other idea if I were you

Joe, ¹( ), I'd make a list of things you need to take with you every day and tape it to your door. ²( ) that you write down appointments in your schedule book with a red pen, and check it several times a day. ³( ) is to download a reminder app on your smartphone.

C 以下は Susan の悩みです。上で学んだことを参考にして、自分で助言を考えてパラグラフを完成させましょう。

"My neighbor's dog sleeps outside and barks all night long. As a result, I can't sleep at night. I'm tired every day, and I often sleep in class." – Susan –

Susan, I have three suggestions that may help you with your problem. First, I recommend that you _____.
If that doesn't work, then I advise you to _____
_____. And if the problem still continues after that, then _____.

4

Sizing Things Up

みなさんは本を買うとき、電子書籍と紙の書籍のどちらを選びますか。紙の本には、電子書籍では再現できない特有の読み心地や質感があるという意見がある一方で、持ち運びやすさや購入しやすさなどの理由から電子書籍を選ぶ人も増えてきています。この Unit では、電子書籍と紙の書籍についての文章を読み、英語で批評や評価を表現する方法を学びましょう。

Warm-Up Questions

次の質問に対して該当する答えに☑をつけましょう。**2.** では 2 つ以上選ぶこともできます。

1. Do you enjoy reading books?

☐ Yes, very much.   ☐ Yes, sometimes.   ☐ No, not very much.

2. What kind of things do you like to read about?

☐ local news   ☐ national news   ☐ world news

☐ sports   ☐ fashion   ☐ other: _____

08
Audio

Reading Books Is Important

A hundred years ago, books were one of our main forms of entertainment. But with the invention of television, the Internet, video games and smartphones,
5▸ it seems that we are reading books less often these days. A recent study of Japanese university students found that over half of them don't read books for pleasure at all. This is unfortunate
10▸ because reading is important. Reading a good book not only gives us pleasure, but it also has many other benefits. It strengthens the brain, builds vocabulary, reduces stress and improves sleep. Many experts say that reading books for pleasure may even help us live longer!

Notes   invention 発明   unfortunate 残念な   benefit 恩恵   strengthen 強くする

Comprehension Questions

本文の内容に合うように、(　　) の中から適切な語句を選びましょう。

1. People are reading less because of (a. technology   b. book prices   c. lack of time).

2. (a. Less than 50%   b. About 50%   c. More than 50%) of Japanese students read books for pleasure.

3. Reading a good book (a. makes the heart stronger   b. takes away stress c. has no health benefits).

Grammar Points

人称代名詞

人称代名詞は、人称（一人称＝話し手、二人称＝聞き手、三人称＝第三者）、数（単数または複数）、主語や目的語などの文法上の働きを表す格に応じて形が変化します。

	単数		複数	
	主格	目的格	主格	目的格
一人称	I	me	we	us
二人称	you	you	you	you
三人称	he/she/it	him/her/it	they	them

※ 代名詞の指す人物の性別が分からない場合や性別を問題としない場合などには、指示対象が単数でも they を用いることがあります。ただし、動詞は複数形と同じ形（○ they are .../ × they is ...）に対応させます。

所有格（「〜の」）と所有代名詞（「〜のもの」）は所有関係を表します。

	単数		複数	
	所有格	所有代名詞	所有格	所有代名詞
一人称	my	mine	our	ours
二人称	your	yours	your	yours
三人称	his/her/its	his/hers/—	their	theirs

Grammar Practice

（　　　）の中から最も適切な語句を選び、○で囲みましょう。

1. I like (your / yours) new T-shirt.

2. "I broke my glasses." "How did you break (it / them)?"

3. "I forgot my dictionary." "You can use (my / mine)."

4. Some of (we / us) speak German.

5. Her hair is really beautiful, isn't (it / she)?

6. They invited my family and (me / I) to the party.

09
Audio

Printed Books Versus E-books

1 The following is an evaluation of printed books and e-books using four important criteria: portability, readability, accessibility and cost.

2 E-books are more portable than printed books. You can carry hundreds of e-books with you on one device that weighs only a few hundred grams. *Advantage: e-books*

5▶ **3** In terms of readability, printed books with small print may damage your eyes. Most e-readers use e-ink. It's easy on the eyes and allows you to read even in bright sunlight. E-books also allow you to change the font size. *Advantage: e-books*

4 With regard to accessibility, you can download e-books in just a few minutes. There's no need to go to the bookstore or library. And most libraries offer e-book 10▶ lending for its members. *Advantage: e-books*

5 As for cost, e-books are cheaper than printed books, and you don't need to buy an e-reader. All you need is a computer, tablet or smartphone. *Advantage: e-books*

Notes criterion (判断・評価の) 基準　easy on~ ~に優しい

Comprehension Questions

本文の内容に関して、次の質問の答えとして適切なものを選びましょう。

1. Which of the following criteria is NOT mentioned?

　a. ease of reading　　b. price　　c. illustrations and photos

2. What is an advantage of e-ink?

　a. It doesn't make your eyes tired.　　b. It changes color in bright sunlight.
　c. It's easy to read in places with poor lighting.

3. Which are more expensive, printed books or e-books?

　a. printed books　b. e-books　c. There's no difference in price.

Writing Strategy

(• 文章内の指示と主題の明示)

(1) 文章内の語句を指す表現 < the following, the former, the latter など >

- Pandas and koalas are both popular animals.
  The former are native to China, and the latter are native to Australia.

- The following is a list of sponsors: XXX, YYY, and ZZZ.

(2) 主題を明示する表現
   < in terms of, with regard to, as for, when it comes to など >

- In terms of location, the hotel is absolutely perfect.

- When it comes to listening to music, I like jazz best.

Paragraph Building

(　　) 内の語句を並び替えて、以下の 4 つの文をそれぞれ完成させましょう。さらに、完成した 4 つの文が 1 つのパラグラフになるように最も適切な順序に並べ、□ に順番を記入しましょう。

How Michelin Awards Stars to Restaurants

☐ • A restaurant that is worth a detour ＿＿＿＿＿＿＿＿＿＿＿＿＿＿＿＿ high
quality receives two stars. (its / cuisine / for / and / excellent)

☐ • Michelin gives three stars to a restaurant that ＿＿＿＿＿＿＿＿＿
＿＿＿＿＿＿ and is worth a special trip. (everything / the / of / best / offers)

☐ • One star means the ＿＿＿＿＿＿＿＿＿＿＿＿＿＿ to stop on your trip.
(place / good / is / restaurant / a)

☐ • Michelin awards restaurants 0 to 3 stars ＿＿＿＿＿＿＿＿＿＿＿＿
＿＿＿＿＿: quality, technique, personality of the chef, value of the food and
consistency. (on / criteria / the / based / following)

　Notes　 worth 〜に値する　detour 遠回り、回り道　consistency 一貫性

A 以下の表は学生の自己評価を表したものです。Jane の自己評価について確認した後、あなた自身についてそれぞれの項目を5段階で評価してみましょう。

5 = Excellent   4 = Very Good   3 = Good   2 = Fair   1 = Poor

Student Self-Evaluation	Jane	You
① Attitude	4	
② Effort	3	
③ Class attendance	4	
④ Studying for tests	3	
⑤ Completing assignments on time	5	
Overall Rating: (① + ② + ③ + ④ + ⑤)÷5	3.8/5	

B Aの表にしたがって、囲みの中の語を使って、Jane の評価について述べたパラグラフを完成させましょう。

attendance   attitude   effort   excellent   herself   studying

Jane has a very good ¹(　　　　　), and she makes a good ²(　　　　　) in class. She has very good class ³(　　　　　). Jane is a good student when it comes to ⁴(　　　　　) for tests, and she's ⁵(　　　　　) when it comes to completing assignments on time. She gives ⁶(　　　　　) an overall rating of 3.8 out of 5.

C Aで考えたことをもとに、あなた自身の評価について1つのパラグラフを書いてみましょう。

I have _____ attitude and I make _____
in class. I have _____
_____
_____
_____.
I give _____ an overall rating of _____.

Unit

5

Mission Accomplished

運動時に飲むものといえば、スポーツドリンクを思い浮かべる人が多いでしょう。日本で初めて発売されたスポーツドリンクは、大塚製薬の「ポカリスエット」と言われています。ポカリスエットは、ある研究員のメキシコでの経験がきっかけとなり誕生しました。この Unit では、ポカリスエットの開発にまつわるエピソードを読み、人の偉大な功績を伝える文章の書き方について学びましょう。

Warm-Up Questions

次の人物たちが 20 世紀に達成したことをそれぞれ右側から選び、線で結びましょう。

Charles Lindbergh ・　　・First to win two Nobel Prizes (1903, 1911)

John Logie Baird ・　　・First successful powered flight (1903)

Marie Curie ・　　・First moving picture on a television (1925)

Ray Tomlinson ・　　・First solo, nonstop transatlantic flight (1927)

The Wright Brothers ・　　・First to climb Mt. Everest (1953)

Sir Edmund Hillary ・　　・First to send email between two computers (1971)
(& Tenzing Norgay)

**10
Audio**

A Product with a Bright Future

In the 1989 hit movie *Back to the Future II*, Marty McFly time-travels between 1985 and 2015. Around the time of
5► filming, Japanese companies were buying American companies, Japanese cars were outselling American cars, and Japanese video games were
10► market leaders. The movie's creators thought the trend would continue well into the future. And so they told the art department to include Japanese things in some of the scenes depicting 2015. One scene shows Marty having a video conference with a co-worker. Interestingly, on a nearby table there is a blue and white can of Pocari Sweat, a Japanese sports drink that
15► remains popular today.

Notes   outsell ～より多く売れる   depict 描く

Comprehension Questions

本文の内容に合うように、（　　）の中から適切なものを選びましょう。

1. In *Back to the Future II*, Marty travels (a. 26　b. 30　c. 36) years into the future.

2. (a. Few people were buying Japanese cars　b. American cars were outselling Japanese cars　c. Japanese cars were popular) in the late 1980s.

3. The scene with the can of Pocari Sweat takes place in (a. 1985　b. 1989　c. 2015).

Grammar Points

→ 過去時制と過去進行形

過去時制（過去形）は、過去のある時点の状態や過去に起こった出来事や行われた動作を表します。

	過去時制（be 動詞）	過去時制（一般動詞）
肯定文	Ken was busy yesterday.	Ken passed the test.
否定文	I wasn't sleepy this morning.	I didn't do my homework last night.
疑問文	Were you there last night?	Did you talk to Sam at the party?

過去進行形は、過去のある時点で進行中の動作や出来事を表します。通常、know, seem, belong, own など
の状態動詞は進行形では用いられません。

	過去進行形
肯定文	Ken was watching TV at that time.
否定文	I wasn't sleeping at ten o'clock last night.
疑問文	Were you playing the piano then?

arrive, become, die, finish, stop などの動詞が過去進行形で
用いられると、動作や出来事が完結に至る途中の段階であっ
たことを意味します。(The train was stopping. vs. The train stopped.)

Grammar Practice

（　　）の中から最も適切な語句を選び、○で囲みましょう。

1. Laura didn't (attend / attending) the meeting.

2. Was she (waited / waiting) for a friend?

3. He (knew / was knowing) the answer.

4. I (lost / was losing) my necklace. I can't find it.

5. "Why didn't you answer my call last night?" "Sorry, I (took / was taking) a shower."

6. Max (broke / was breaking) his leg when he fell down.

11
Audio

A Great "Solution"

■ During a business trip to Mexico in the 1970s, Rokuro Harima, a researcher for a pharmaceutical company, became ill. He was suffering from diarrhea and dehydration. Doctors told Harima to rehydrate with soda drinks such as cola. While in hospital, however,
5► he noticed that doctors were rehydrating themselves by drinking pouches of IV (intravenous) solution. This gave Harima the idea to develop a tasty, "drinkable" IV.

② In the laboratory, Harima and his team of researchers developed dozens of samples, but they all tasted too bitter. They finally solved the problem by adding a little citrus juice powder, and produced two samples with different sugar levels. In those days,
10► there was a growing interest in health, sports and outdoor leisure activities in Japan. So, after drinking both samples while climbing a mountain in Tokushima Prefecture, Harima and his team decided that the less sugary version went better with exercise. The company named the sports drink Pocari Sweat, and began selling it in 1980.

Notes pharmaceutical company 製薬会社   diarrhea 下痢   dehydration 脱水症状   IV solution 点滴液

Comprehension Questions

本文の内容に関して、次の質問の答えとして適切なものを選びましょう。

1. Why did Mr. Harima go to Mexico?

   a. for business   b. to visit friends   c. for medical treatment

2. Where did Mr. Harima get the idea for the drink?

   a. in a laboratory   b. on a mountain   c. in a hospital

3. What did the researchers add to the drink in order to remove the bitter taste?

   a. sugar   b. citrus juice powder   c. salt

Writing Strategy

> 同じ表現の重複を避ける

文章や発話の中で、同じ対象や事柄が常に同一の表現で表されるとは限りません。一度出てきた表現は、代名詞 (he, she, it, they など)、指示表現 (this, that, these, those, there, so など)、別の語句などを用いて言い換えられたり、省略されたりすることが多くあります。

- Kenji took off his (= Kenji's) jacket and hung it (= his jacket) on the hook.

- Naomi came to the party wearing a white silk gown. Her beautiful dress (= Naomi's white silk gown) caught the attention of everyone there (= at the party).

- Oliver doesn't play tennis now, but he used to play tennis.

Paragraph Building

(   ) 内の語句を並び替えて、以下の 4 つの文をそれぞれ完成させましょう。さらに、完成した 4 つの文が 1 つのパラグラフになるように最も適切な順序に並べ、□に順番を記入しましょう。

A Remarkable Achievement

- [ ] • But winning _____.
(truly / 28 / incredible / is / medals)

- [ ] • _____ 23 gold medals, 3 silver medals and 2 bronze medals. (time, / during / he / that / won)

- [ ] • Winning an Olympic medal _____ for any athlete. (achievement / is / sports / great / a)

- [ ] • That's what Michael Phelps did _____ the American Olympic swim team between 2000 and 2016.
(for / he / swimming / when / was)

37

Paragraph Writing

A 以下の功績や成果をそれぞれ１～３にしたがって分類し、番号を□に記入しましょう。

    1 = school or study-based
    2 = work-related
    3 = extracurricular activity

Notes extracurricular activity 課外活動　promotion 昇進

☐ completed a university internship
☐ helped train other workers
☐ passed Eiken level 2 or higher
☐ received a promotion
☐ supervised other staff members
☐ won a city, prefectural or national competition or award

☐ did important volunteer work
☐ maintained a high G.P.A.
☐ passed a university entrance test
☐ studied overseas
☐ was a team captain
☐ won a school contest or award
☐ worked part-time while studying

B 囲みの中の語句を使って、以下のモデルパラグラフを完成させましょう。

> didn't　　fell　　practiced　　named　　supported　　was

I began playing soccer at a very early age—four or five years old, I think. I
¹(　　　　　　　　) in love with the game, and ²(　　　　　　　　) almost every
day. In my first year of high school, I became a member of the soccer team.
I ³(　　　　　　　) play in many games, but I practiced hard, ⁴(　　　　　　　)
my teammates, and gradually became better and better. Then, in my third year,
the coach ⁵(　　　　　　　　) me team captain. It ⁶(　　　　　　　) a great
honor and accomplishment for me.

C Bのモデルパラグラフを参考にして、あなた自身が達成したことについて、５つ以上の文でできる
だけ詳しく説明してみましょう。

This Really Happened

海外旅行や長距離移動の際の移動手段として当たり前のように利用されている飛行機は、もともと軍用機として開発されました。その後、貨物機や旅客機などの民間輸送機として実用化が進められ、様々な過程を経て、現在のような安全で快適な乗り物になりました。この Unit では旅客機にまつわる文章を読み、英語で出来事を正確に伝えるための練習をしましょう。

Warm-Up Questions

次の質問に対して **1.** は該当する答えに ☑ をつけ、**2.** と **3.** は英語で答えましょう。

1. Which of these kinds of transportation have you taken? Check the boxes.

   ☐ airplane ☐ Shinkansen ☐ helicopter ☐ ship ☐ horse

   ☐ monorail ☐ rickshaw ☐ ferry ☐ cable car ☐ motorcycle

2. What kind of transportation would you like to take someday? _____

3. Which would you prefer, traveling to Hawaii by ship or by airplane?

   I'd prefer going by _____ because _____.

**12
Audio**

The Birth of Commercial Aviation

On New Year's Day, 1914, the world's first commercial airline service began, operating between St. Petersburg and Tampa, Florida. The 34-kilometer flight across the bay took only 23 minutes, compared to two hours needed to

5▸ cross the bay by steamship and 20 hours to drive around it by car. The airplane held only one pilot and one passenger side-by-side on a single wooden seat. The plane

10▸ had a top speed of 103 kilometers per hour, and flew about 15 meters above the water. A one-way trip cost $5, or about $125 in today's dollars. The St. Petersburg-Tampa

15▸ Airboat Line operated for less than four months.

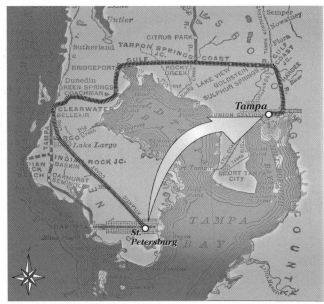

©National Air and Space Museum

| Notes | commercial 商用の   aviation 航空   steamship 汽船、蒸気船   passenger 乗客 |

本文の内容に合うように、(　　)の中から適切なものを選びましょう。

1. It took (a. two   b. twelve   c. twenty) hours to drive from St. Petersburg to Tampa.

2. The passenger sat (a. behind   b. beside   c. in front of) the pilot on the airplane.

3. The airplane flew (a. 23   b. 34   c. 103) kilometers across the bay.

Grammar Points

時や場所を表す前置詞

前置詞は後ろの名詞と結びついて、時間や空間などに関する情報を表します。

前置詞	時を表す	場所を表す
in	in the morning / in December / in 2010	in the room / in the city / in Japan
on	on Monday / on the weekend	on the floor / on the beach
at	at midnight / at 10 p.m.	at home / at the hotel
around	around noon / around 1980	around the corner / around the world
between	between Monday and Wednesday	between the two stations
from ... to ~	from 9:00 to 5:00	from Osaka to Tokyo

対義関係にある前置詞	
over the bridge ⟷ under the bridge	in front of the house ⟷ behind the house
above sea level ⟷ below sea level	into the room ⟷ out of the room

時の終点を示す前置詞		期間を示す前置詞	
till/until	till tomorrow / until next year	for	for an hour / for three years
by	by tomorrow / by next year	during	during the day / during the holidays

※ till (until) は「〜まで（ずっと）」という意味で、継続する行為や出来事が終了する時点を示します。by は「〜までに」という意味で、期限を表します。for の後には時間の長さを示す語句が続き、during の後には特定の期間を表す名称が続きます。

Grammar Practice

(   ) の中から最も適切な語句を選び、○で囲みましょう。

1. The store closes (at / for) 9:00.

2. The restrooms are (in / on) the second floor.

3. I'm free (between / from) 10:30 and 12:00.

4. I need to finish my homework (until / by) tomorrow.

5. George fell asleep (for / during) the meeting.

6. He has traveled (to / around) the world.

**13
Audio**

Miracle on the Hudson

■1 On January 15, 2009 at approximately 3:25 p.m., US Airways flight 1549 took off from New York's LaGuardia Airport for Charlotte, North Carolina. On board were 150 passengers and 5 crew members, including Captain Chesley Sullenberger. About 40 seconds into the flight, Sullenberger said to his co-pilot Jeffrey Skiles, "What a view of the Hudson today." Just over half a minute later, the airplane flew into a flock of Canada geese. Both engines died.

■2 An air traffic controller directed Sullenberger to return to LaGuardia. Sullenberger responded, "Unable." The captain then received permission to land at Teterboro Airport in nearby New Jersey. He first responded, "Yes," then seconds later, "We can't do it. …We're gonna be in the Hudson." At approximately 3:29 p.m., Sullenberger announced, "This is the captain. Brace for impact." Ninety seconds later, the plane landed in the middle of the river. Everyone survived, and the "Miracle on the Hudson" became part of aviation history.

Notes a flock of 〜の一群   Canada goose カナダ雁   brace for impact 衝撃に備えよ   survive 生き延びる

Comprehension Questions

本文の内容に関して、次の質問の答えとして適切なものを選びましょう。

1. How long after takeoff did the airplane strike the flock of birds?

   a. about 40 seconds   b. about 70 seconds   c. about 90 seconds

2. Why didn't Captain Sullenberger try to land at Teterboro Airport?

   a. He didn't receive permission.   b. The co-pilot was against the idea.
   c. He didn't think a successful landing was possible.

3. Where did the airplane land?

   a. on Lake Hudson   b. on the Hudson River   c. in Hudson Park

Writing Strategy

(→ 直接話法と間接話法)

発言された言葉をそのまま引用して伝える方法を直接話法といい、伝達する話し手の言葉で言い直した方法を間接話法といいます。間接話法の場合、主節の時制に応じて伝達部分の動詞の時制を変化させ、伝達する話し手の視点に合わせて代名詞などの要素を変化させる必要があります。

直接話法
John said, "I'm hungry now."
間接話法
John said that he was hungry then.

直接話法
John said to me, "Have you finished the report?"
間接話法
John asked me if/whether I had finished the report.

Paragraph Building

(   ) 内の語句を並び替えて、以下の4つの文をそれぞれ完成させましょう。さらに、完成した4つの文が1つのパラグラフになるように最も適切な順序に並べ、□に順番を記入しましょう。

A Great Historical Event

□ • Bell's first words were, "Mr. Watson, come here—_____."
(see / I / to / want / you)

□ • Watson then went _____ Bell's sentence.
(laboratory / to / repeated / the / and)

□ • From the laboratory above his home in Boston, _____
_____ Thomas Watson, who was in a different room.
(spoke / assistant / his / Bell / to)

□ • On March 10, 1876, Alexander Graham Bell _____
_____. (made / first-ever / the / call / telephone)

43

Paragraph Writing

A 以下のイラストが表す出来事の名前をそれぞれ選択肢から選び、記入しましょう。

accident / concert / festival / homestay / party / sports event / trip / wedding

1. _____ 
2. _____ 
3. _____ 
4. _____

5. _____
6. _____ 
7. _____ 
8. _____ 

B 囲みの中の語句を使って、以下のモデルパラグラフを完成させましょう。

| after   around   at   in   on   until |

¹(　　　　　　　) June 1, 2019, I attended my older sister Amy's wedding. She married her high school sweetheart Tom. It was a church wedding ²(　　　　　) Hawaii, with about 50 guests. ³(　　　　　　) the end of the ceremony, the priest said to Amy and Tom, "I now pronounce you man and wife." I cried with joy. ⁴(　　　　　　) the wedding, there was a big party on the beach. Everyone ate and danced ⁵(　　　　) a big fire ⁶(　　　　　　) midnight. It was a great memory for me. **Notes** priest 司祭　pronounce 宣言する

C Bのモデルパラグラフを参考にして、あなた自身の思い出に残っている出来事や経験を1つ取り上げ、説明してみましょう。

Unit
7

Solving a Problem

Every Problem Has a Solution

日々の生活の中で、待つことが必要になる場面は意外に多くあります。コンビニやスーパーのレジ、遊園地、病院など、あらゆる場所で待ち時間は発生します。サービス産業では、待ち時間自体を短縮するための工夫に加えて、顧客にとって待ち時間を退屈に感じさせないための様々なアイデアが考案・実践されています。この Unit では問題解決に関する英語表現を学びましょう。

Warm-Up Questions

次の質問に対してそれぞれ英語で答えましょう。

1. List 4 places where people often have to wait in line. (ex. convenience stores)

   _____ / _____ / _____ / _____

2. What is the longest time you have ever waited in line? _____

   What were you waiting for? _____

3. What do you usually do while waiting in line? _____

45

14
Audio

Is the Elevator Ever Going to Come?

In the 1950s, a tall office building in Manhattan had a problem. Workers complained that they had to wait a long time for an elevator when they arrived in the morning, took their lunch break and left at night. Engineers said they couldn't do anything to speed up the service, so the building
5▶ manager asked his staff for ideas that might solve the problem. One staff member pointed out that people were probably just bored. He thought the manager should put large mirrors near the
10▶ elevators so that people could look at themselves and others while waiting. The manager took the worker's advice, and complaints dropped to nearly
15▶ zero.

Notes   complain 苦情を言う   solve 解決する   bored 退屈した   complaint 苦情

Comprehension Questions

本文の内容に合うように、(　　)の中から適切な語句を選びましょう。

1. The workers complained about (a. the wait time for the elevators   b. the size of the elevators   c. the small number of elevators).

2. Engineers were unable to (a. install new elevators   b. find any problems with the elevators   c. make the elevators go faster).

3. (a. Many   b. Few   c. No) people complained after the manager installed the mirrors.

Grammar Points

助動詞

＜助動詞＋動詞の原形＞は、忠告・義務・提案や話し手の確信の度合いなどを表します。

忠告・義務・提案		話し手の確信の度合い
You could go.	弱	The report might be ready tomorrow.
You should/ought to go.	↑	The report may be ready tomorrow.
You had better go.	↓	The report should/ought to be ready tomorrow.
You must/have to go.	強	The report must/has to be ready tomorrow.

以下の助動詞の疑問文と否定文は特に意味に注意しましょう。

疑問文	否定文
May/Could I ask you a question?（許可）	You must not go.（禁止）
Can you wait a minute?（依頼）	You can't/may not go.（不許可）
Could you wait a minute?（丁寧な依頼）	It can't/couldn't be true.（推量）
Do I have to go with them?（義務）	You don't have to go.（不必要）

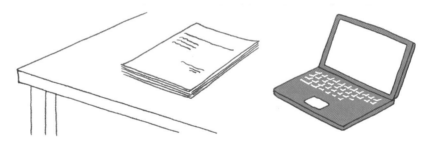

Grammar Practice

（　　）の中から最も適切な語句を選び、○で囲みましょう。

1. My father (have to / has to) take the medicine three times a day.

2. I'm sorry, but you (can't / don't) smoke here.

3. (Do / Must) I have to pay in advance?

4. You (must not / don't have to) enter the area without permission.

5. "I didn't have breakfast today." "You (must / can't) be hungry now."

6. We left early so that we (must / could) arrive there on time.

15
Audio

Please Wait

1 Waiting in line isn't something people look forward to or do for fun. Yet many people spend one or even two years of their lives doing it. At first, one might think that long lines are good for business. In most cases, however, the opposite is true. A long and unpleasant wait can damage the way
5► customers view a business or a brand. It may cause customers to leave a line or not enter it at all. And some customers might never come back again.

2 Luckily, theme parks, museums, movie theaters, etc. have found a way to shorten lines by charging customers for skipping or moving up in the line. Another technique that businesses use to solve the waiting time problem is distraction. Mirrors beside
10► elevators, television screens at airports and hospitals, and magazines in dental clinics all help to make the time spent waiting go by faster. And customers have their own secret weapon to kill time while waiting—their smartphone.

> **Notes** charge 料金をとる distraction 気晴らし secret weapon 秘密兵器 kill time 時間をつぶす

Comprehension Questions

本文の内容に関して、次の質問の答えとして適切なものを選びましょう。

1. What is generally true about waiting in line?

　a. It's good for business.　　b. People look forward to it.
　c. It may harm businesses.

2. What can customers do in order to enter a museum more quickly?

　a. pay extra　　b. start a new line　　c. stand closer together

3. What is the purpose of creating a distraction?

　a. to reduce waiting time　　b. to skip or move up in a line
　c. to help pass the time

Writing Strategy

(• 無生物主語)

英語では、原因・理由、手段、条件となる物事を主語として、それが人を「〜する（させる）」という形式がよく用いられます。

- Because of the storm, I couldn't go to the ceremony.

  ▶ The storm prevented me from going to the ceremony.

- If you take this medicine, you will feel better.

  ▶ Taking this medicine will make you feel better.

  ▶ This medicine will make you feel better.

Paragraph Building

(　　) 内の語句を並び替えて、以下の 4 つの文をそれぞれ完成させましょう。さらに、完成した 4 つの文が 1 つのパラグラフになるように最も適切な順序に並べ、□ に順番を記入しましょう。

The Waiting Game

- □ But contrary to what you might expect, these _____
  _____. (times / usually / wait / overestimated / are)

- □ Some amusement parks tell their customers how long _____
  _____ for various attractions. (to / they / expect / wait / can)

- □ As a result, _____ that they arrived at
  the front of the line "ahead of schedule."
  (pleasantly / the / surprised / is / customer)

- □ For example, a customer faced with a long wait time of one hour may only
  _____ for 45 minutes. (to / line / have / stand / in)

  Notes be overestimated 過大に見積もられる be pleasantly surprised 良い意味で驚かされる、嬉しい驚きだ

A 以下の点と点を結んで、環境保護のための方法について述べた文を完成させましょう。

1.	At supermarkets, etc., say NO to	…in the same garbage bag.	Recycle them.
2.	Turn off the lights	…when you brush your teeth.	Limit the time to 10 minutes.
3.	Don't put newspapers, plastic, glass, etc.	…plastic bags.	Pick it up and carry it away.
4.	Don't leave garbage	…long showers.	Bring your own cloth ones.
5.	Don't run the water	…when leaving a room.	Don't leave them on.
6.	Try not to take	…in parks, on beaches, etc.	Turn it off.

B Aの意見とあなた自身の考えをもとに、環境を守る方法について述べたパラグラフを完成させましょう。それぞれの文で異なる助動詞を用いて書いてみましょう。

We can all do our part to protect the environment by doing some very simple things. Here are four examples. First, when we go shopping, we should say NO to plastic bags. We can bring our own cloth bags. Second, _____

_____.

Third, _____

_____. One more thing we _____

_____.

Ideas:

Let Me Make It Clear

アメリカ合衆国大統領選挙は、米国の大統領を決めるために4年ごとに行われる選挙です。全世界の人々の関心を集める選挙ですが、日本とは大きく異なる選挙方法で行われるため、多くの人にとって馴染みのない点もあると思います。この Unit では、アメリカ合衆国大統領選挙の仕組みについて述べた文章を読み、英語でものごとを明確に説明する方法を学びましょう。

Warm-Up Questions

次の質問に対してそれぞれ英語で答えましょう。

1. Who is the current president of the United States? _____

2. Can you name four other U.S. presidents?

   _____ / _____ / _____ / _____

3. What is the capital of the United States? _____

4. Where does the president live and work in the nation's capital?

   _____

16
Audio

U.S. Presidents: FAQs

Who can become president of the United States?

1   It is often said that in America, anyone can become president. But
5►that's not really true. There are actually three requirements.

What are the requirements?

2   First, the president must be a natural-born citizen—a U.S. citizen at birth. Second, they must be at least 35 years
10►old. Third, they must have lived in the United States for 14 years or more.

How long can a person be president?

3   The president is elected to a four-year term, with a limit of two terms. However, if a president serves less than two years in a term, the next president may serve up to ten years.

Notes FAQs (Frequently Asked Questions) よくある質問   requirement 必要条件
natural-born その土地で生まれた   term 任期

Comprehension Questions

本文の内容に合うように、(　　)の中から適切な語句を選びましょう。

1. The president of the United States must (a. have lived in the U.S. all of their life b. have native English language ability c. be born a U.S. citizen).

2. There is (a. a minimum age requirement b. a maximum age requirement c. no age requirement) to become president of the United States.

3. One presidential term is (a. 2 years b. 4 years c. 8 years) long.

Grammar Points

疑問代名詞と疑問副詞

「誰」または「何」といった情報を尋ねるには疑問代名詞を用い、時、場所、理由、様態、程度などの情報を尋ねる場合は疑問副詞を用いて疑問文を作ります。疑問代名詞が文中で主語の働きをする場合を除いて、疑問文は肯定文と語順が異なるので注意しましょう。

疑問代名詞	意味	例文
who	誰が	Who loves him?
	誰・誰を・誰に	Who does he love?
what	何が	What happened in the kitchen?
	何・何を・何に	What did she do in the kitchen?

疑問副詞	意味	例文
when	いつ	When did they leave the room?
where	どこで・どこに・どこへ	Where did you see him?
why	なぜ	Why does John study Japanese?
how	どのように、どう	How did you get here?
how +形容詞 / 副詞	どのくらい	How hot is the water?

Grammar Practice

( )の中から最も適切な語句を選び、○で囲みましょう。

1. (Who / When) wrote this letter?

2. Where (you wrote / did you write) this letter?

3. Why (did you / were you) late this morning?

4. (What / When) did you find in the room?

5. (What / How) did you find it?

6. (How is it far / How far is it) to the airport?

17 Audio

How to Become President of the USA

1 American presidential elections are held every four years. You may think that the candidate who receives the most votes wins, but that's not necessarily true. Then how does the U.S. president get elected?

2 When Americans vote, they're actually voting for people called "electors" in their state. These people form the Electoral College. It consists of 538 electors. The number of electoral votes of each state depends on its population. States with small populations such as Alaska and Montana have three electoral votes. On the other hand, California, the state with the largest population, has 55 votes. In a presidential election, the winning candidate in 48 states gets all of the electoral votes for that state. The same is true for Washington, D.C. Nebraska and Maine split electoral votes.

3 So, who wins? The candidate who receives a majority of the 538 electoral votes—in other words, 270 or more—becomes President of the United States.

Notes candidate 候補者   elect 選出する   vote 投票する   Electoral College 選挙人団   split 分ける、割り振る

Comprehension Questions

本文の内容に関して、次の質問の答えとして適切なものを選びましょう。

1. What is the Electoral College?

　a. a group of candidates　b. a group of electors　c. a group of states

2. Why does California get more electoral votes than Alaska?

　a. It's part of the Electoral College.　b. It has a larger economy.
　c. It has more people.

3. If a candidate wins the electoral votes in California, how many more electoral votes will they need to become president of the Unites States?

　a. 215　　b. 270　　c. 483

Writing Strategy

(→ 部分否定と言い換え)

(1) 部分否定を表す表現

< not always, not necessarily, not all, not every など >

（全体否定） • It's never a good idea to stay up all night before an exam.

（部分否定） • It's not always a good idea to tell the truth.

（全体否定） • No one attended the meeting yesterday.

（部分否定） • Not everyone likes the new teacher.

(2) 言い換えを表す表現

< namely, in other words, that is (to say) など >

• The research focuses on the elderly, namely people aged 65 and over.

Paragraph Building

(　　　) 内の語句を並び替えて、以下の 4 つの文をそれぞれ完成させましょう。さらに、完成した 4 つの文が 1 つのパラグラフになるように最も適切な順序に並べ、□に順番を記入しましょう。

This Artist Paints with Her Eyes

□ • Unable to move her arms, Ezekiel uses specialized technology to track _____ _____ and control a cursor on a screen.
(her / of / movement / eyes / the)

□ • There are millions of talented painters in the world, _____ _____ with their eyes like artist Sarah Ezekiel.
(everyone / paint / can / not / but)

□ • _____, she uses her eyes as her "brush" and the screen as her "canvas." (another / it / to / way / put)

□ • "_____ with their eyes?" you might ask.
(can / paint / anyone / how / possibly)

55

A 以下は健康に関する質問表です。Bob の回答を確認した後、あなた自身について該当する答えを選び、☑をつけましょう。

HEALTH SURVEY	Bob		You	
How is your health condition?	☐ excellent ☐ good ☐ fair	☑ poor	☐ excellent ☐ good ☐ fair	☐ poor
Do you often get colds?	☑ Yes	☐ No	☐ Yes	☐ No
Do you often feel tired?	☑ Yes	☐ No	☐ Yes	☐ No
Do you often have trouble sleeping?	☐ Yes	☑ No	☐ Yes	☐ No
Is your life stressful?	☐ Yes	☑ No	☐ Yes	☐ No
Do you exercise regularly?	☐ Yes	☑ No	☐ Yes	☐ No
Do you usually eat breakfast?	☐ Yes	☑ No	☐ Yes	☐ No
Do you eat vegetables every day?	☐ Yes	☑ No	☐ Yes	☐ No
Do you eat lots of sweets/junk food?	☑ Yes	☐ No	☐ Yes	☐ No

B A で確認した Bob の回答をもとに、囲みの中の語句を使って、Bob の健康状態について述べたパラグラフを完成させましょう。

breakfast	eating habits	poor	positive	stressful	tired

Bob thinks he's in ¹(   ) health. He often gets colds and feels ²(   ), and he doesn't exercise regularly. He also has poor ³(   ). Namely, he doesn't usually eat ⁴(   ), he doesn't eat vegetables every day, and he eats lots of sweets and junk food. On the ⁵(   ) side, he doesn't have trouble sleeping, and his life isn't ⁶(   ).

C A で回答した内容をもとに、あなた自身の健康状態について 1 つのパラグラフを書いてみましょう。

I think my health is _____. Let me explain what I mean. _____

_____

_____

_____

_____

_____

Don't You See It My Way?

安くて、美味しくて、注文してからすぐに食べられるファストフードは、その手軽さゆえに子供から大人まで多くの人に親しまれています。魅力的な点が多いファストフードですが、みなさんはその栄養面について考えてみたことはありますか。この Unit では、ファストフードについて述べた文章を読み、英語で説得力のある文章を書くための方法を学びましょう。

Warm-Up Questions

次の質問に対して **1.** は該当するものに☑をつけ、**2.** と **3.** は英語で答えましょう。

1. How often do you eat fast food?

   ☐ a few times a year   ☐ once or twice a month

   ☐ once or twice a week   ☐ three or more times a week

2. What's your favorite fast food restaurant? _____

3. What are your three favorite fast foods?

   _____ / _____ / _____

18
Audio

Japanese Eating Habits over the Years

For religious reasons, Japanese people mostly avoided eating meat after the arrival of Buddhism in the 6th century. They ate mainly rice, seafood, vegetables and pickles, and very little fat and animal products. That all changed with the revolutionary Meiji period beginning in 1868. During that time, the eating habits of Japanese people
5▸ slowly started shifting. They began to eat meat again, as well as food from Western countries such as potatoes and cheese. Later, in 1971, McDonald's opened its
10▸ first restaurant in Japan, and the phrase "fast food" became popular. People have been "lovin' it" ever since.

Notes　avoid 避ける　Buddhism 仏教　pickle 漬物　revolutionary 革新的な、革命的な

Comprehension Questions

本文の内容に合うように、（　　）の中から適切な語句を選びましょう。

1. Most Japanese people didn't eat meat (a. before the 6th century　b. after the arrival of Buddhism　c. during the Meiji period).

2. Japanese people started eating Western food (a. before　b. after　c. during) the Meiji era.

3. (a. "Fast food"　b. "Lovin' it"　c. "Big Mac") became a popular phrase in Japan in the 1970s.

Grammar Points

to 不定詞・動名詞を目的語にとる動詞

to 不定詞を目的語にとるか、動名詞を目的語にとるかは動詞によって異なります。どちらを目的語にとるかによって意味に違いが出る場合もあるので注意しましょう。

動詞 (V)	目的語 (O)		例文
agree, expect, hope, promise, want など	to 不定詞 ◯	動名詞 ×	• I want to leave now. • Paul promised to help us.
avoid, enjoy, finish, give up, mind など	to 不定詞 ×	動名詞 ◯	• Beth enjoys listening to jazz. • I finished reading the book.
to 不定詞・動名詞のいずれも目的語にとれるもの begin, continue, like, prefer, start など	to 不定詞 ◯	動名詞 ◯	• I prefer to work alone. • I prefer working alone. ※ to 不定詞の場合も動名詞の場合も基本的に同じ意味を表します。
to 不定詞と動名詞で意味が異なるもの forget, regret, remember など	to 不定詞 ◯	動名詞 ◯	• Don't forget to go there. • I'll never forget going there. ※ to 不定詞は「（これから）〜することを…する」、動名詞は「〜したことを…する」という意味になります。

Grammar Practice

( ) の中から最も適切な語句を選び、◯で囲みましょう。

1. I hope (to see / seeing) you again soon.

2. You should give up (to smoke / smoking).

3. He just (started / finished) to read the book.

4. I don't (mind / want) living near a busy road.

5. Nancy doesn't remember (to meet / meeting) him before.

6. Please remember (to call / calling) me when you arrive at the airport.

19
Audio

Fast Food—A Lifesaver or a Life Breaker?

1 Thank goodness for fast food! After all, who doesn't like hamburgers, French fries, fried chicken, pizza and donuts? Fast food is delicious, inexpensive and fast—perfect for busy people, or people who just don't like cooking, right? It's really a lifesaver, isn't it? …Think again. Fast food may shorten
5▶ your life by as many as 10 years!

2 Most fast food contains lots of fat, sugar, salt, preservatives and unhealthy calories. This can lead to heart disease, cancer, obesity and many other health problems. Furthermore, fast food may also affect your brain. Too much fast food limits your ability to think and create new memories. It may also lead to memory loss.

10▶ 3 So the next time you find yourself waiting in line to buy a burger and fries or a chocolate donut, think about how your choice could affect your health. You might want to walk away and find something healthier.

Notes Thank goodness よかった、助かった   lifesaver 困ったときに助けになる人（もの）   preservative 防腐剤   cancer がん   obesity 肥満

Comprehension Questions

本文の内容に関して、次の質問の答えとして適切なものを選びましょう。

1. Which fast food does the passage mention?

   a. pizza   b. hotdog   c. chocolate muffin

2. What does the author suggest people do before buying fast food?

   a. check the price   b. think about the health risk   c. count the calories

3. Which statement about fast food does the author agree with?

   a. It's a lifesaver.   b. The disadvantages outweigh the advantages.
   c. It's an excellent choice for busy people.

Writing Strategy

→ 情報を追加する

(1) 等位接続詞として働くもの < and, or, nor など >

- Jim is not an actor or a singer.
  （not A or B は neither A nor B の解釈になる点に注意）

(2) 相関接続詞・群接続詞として働くもの
  < not only A but (also) B, A as well as B など >

- Rebecca is not only a famous pianist but also a great teacher.

(3) 前置詞として働くもの < in addition to, besides など >

- In addition to being a famous pianist, Rebecca is a great teacher.

(4) 副詞語句として働くもの < moreover, furthermore, in addition, also など >

- Rebecca is a famous pianist. Moreover, she is a great teacher.

Paragraph Building

(　　　) 内の語句を並び替えて、以下の 4 つの文をそれぞれ完成させましょう。さらに、完成した 4 つの文が 1 つのパラグラフになるように最も適切な順序に並べ、□ に順番を記入しましょう。

Get Swimming

□ • Moreover, _____ to maintain a healthy weight, a healthy heart and healthy lungs. (way / is / great / a / swimming)

□ • _____, but did you know that swimming is also one of the best forms of exercise?
(swimming / people / of / millions / enjoy)

□ • For these reasons, swimming is a highly recommended form of fitness _____ _____. (of / ages / people / all / for)

□ • It builds strength and endurance like running or lifting weights, but _____ _____ joints. (muscles / stress / and / on / without)

Notes　lung 肺　endurance 持久力　joint 関節

61

A 以下は富士登山に関連する考えや意見を表した語句です。知らない語句があれば意味を調べましょう。

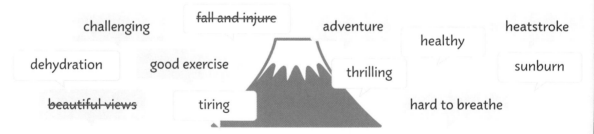

challenging   ~~fall and injure~~   adventure   healthy   heatstroke

dehydration   good exercise   thrilling   sunburn

~~beautiful views~~   tiring   hard to breathe

B A の各語句の表す内容が下の表のどちらの項目に当てはまるかを考え、それぞれ該当する方に記入しましょう。

Reasons for climbing Mt. Fuji	Reasons for NOT climbing Mt. Fuji
• beautiful views	• fall and injure
•	•
•	•
•	•
•	•
•	•

C あなたの友人が一緒に 8 月に富士登山をしたいと言っているとします。あなたはそれが賢明ではないと考え、友人に考えを改めるように説得するためのメールを送ることにします。上で考えたこととあなた自身の考えをもとにメールの文面を完成させましょう。

I understand why you want to climb Mt. Fuji. It would be a thrilling adventure, and we could see beautiful views from the top. In addition, _____
_____.
However, climbing Mt. Fuji in summer can be very dangerous. We might fall and injure ourselves. Moreover, _____.
Besides, _____.
Remember, we're not experienced climbers, so it would be very risky to try and make the climb. Let's think of something else to do that's not only fun but also safe.

One Thing Leads to Another

ソーシャルメディアとは、インターネット上で利用者同士が情報を発信したり、共有したりすることを特徴としたメディアで、代表的なものに Twitter などの SNS、YouTube などの動画共有サイト、LINE などのメッセージ・チャットアプリがあります。この Unit では、ソーシャルメディアの恩恵や影響について考えながら、原因や結果を英語で表現する方法を学びましょう。

Warm-Up Questions

次の質問に対して該当する答えを選び、☑ をつけましょう。2 つ以上選ぶこともできます。

1. Which of the following social media sites/apps do you use?

   ☐ Facebook　　☐ Twitter　☐ YouTube　　☐ Instagram

   ☐ Messenger　☐ LINE　　☐ TikTok　　☐ Other: _____

2. Why do you use social media?

   ☐ To know what friends are doing　　☐ To stay up-to-date with news

   ☐ To find funny or entertaining content　☐ Other: _____

20
Audio

Social Media

Over the past 20 years, social media has greatly changed the way we communicate. Thanks to social media, we are able to share
5▸ information, ideas, photos and videos—quickly, cheaply and in real time. Social media enables us to keep in touch with family, friends, classmates and business partners, and to connect with people with the same interests or concerns. For university students, social media has not only changed the way they communicate, but the way in which they live, study and learn.
10▸ It has also become an important part of their success and future growth.

Notes   keep in touch 連絡を取り合う

Comprehension Questions

本文の内容に合うように、(　　) の中から適切な語句を選びましょう。

1. Social media has changed the way people (a. shop b. travel c. communicate).

2. Social media brings together people with the same interests or (a. worries b. information c. skills).

3. The way students live, study and (a. think b. learn c. work) has changed because of social media.

Grammar Points

現在完了

< have/has + 過去分詞 >の形で、現在までに完了した行為やその結果を表したり、過去のある時点から現在まで継続している状態や現在までの経験を表したりします。

She has lost her passport.

過去　　　　　現在　　　　　未来

She lost her passport.

- Sam **has gone** to Vancouver. — 結果
- I **haven't done** my homework yet. — 完了
- **Have** you ever **seen** this movie? — 経験
- She **has been** sick since last week. — 継続

< for + 期間 >は「～の間」、< since + 過去の時点 >は「～以来」という意味を表します。

- I haven't seen Mark **for** { three days / several years / ages / a long time }.
- I haven't seen Mark **since** { this morning / yesterday / his wedding / he left New York }.

Grammar Practice

(　　)の中から最も適切な語句を選び、○で囲みましょう。

1. (Have / Has) Laura arrived yet?

2. They have just (began / begun) the meeting.

3. Have you (ever visited / visited ever) the museum?

4. Sales of new cars have increased (for / since) the last few months.

5. Naomi has changed a lot (for / since) high school.

6. Emma has read the novel (twice / two years ago).

21 Audio

Benefits of Social Media for University Students

1   Many students say that, because of social media, their lives have changed in a number of positive ways. It has given them more confidence in themselves, brought them closer to family and friends, and made them more aware of important social issues.

2   Social media has also had a positive effect on the way students study and learn. Thanks to social media networks, online classes and distance learning have become increasingly popular with students around the world. And messaging and video chat tools enable students to work on group projects without in-person meetings.

3   Finally, social media helps students prepare for life after university. Students can research companies, upload their résumés, apply for jobs, and have online job interviews. And, thanks to social media, building social networks with co-workers and business partners has never been easier.

4   In conclusion, social media is a powerful tool. When used well, it can have a positive effect on students' everyday lives, their education and their future.

Notes   aware 意識して   social issue 社会問題   résumé 履歴書   apply 応募する   interview 面接

Comprehension Questions

本文の内容に関して、次の質問の答えとして適切なものを選びましょう。

1. What has social media given many students?

   a. more self-control   b. more friends   c. more social awareness

2. What are messaging and video chat tools useful for?

   a. in-person discussions   b. student collaborations   c. tracking locations

3. What does social media help prepare students for?

   a. their daily lives   b. their education   c. their careers

Writing Strategy

原因・理由と結果を表す

(1) 原因・理由を表す接続詞 (because, since, as など)

- George failed the test because he was lazy.

  結果 　　　　　　　　 原因・理由

(2) 原因・理由を表す前置詞 (because of, due to, thanks to, as a result of など)

- George failed the test because of his laziness.

  結果 　　　　　　　　 原因・理由

(3) 結果を表す等位接続詞 (so)

- George was lazy, so he failed the test.

  原因・理由 　　　　 結果

(4) 結果を表す副詞語句 (as a result, therefore, consequently など)

- George was lazy. As a result, he failed the test.

  原因・理由 　　　　　　　 結果

Notes　lazy 怠けて、怠惰な
laziness 怠惰

Paragraph Building

(　　) 内の語句を並び替えて、以下の４つの文をそれぞれ完成させましょう。さらに、完成した４つの文が１つのパラグラフになるように最も適切な順序に並べ、□に順番を記入しましょう。

Why People Get Headaches

- First, _____ from things like work, family
  matters or money. (stress / are / many / due to / headaches)

- People _____.
  (headaches / reasons / get / several / for)

- Finally, products such as paint, bug killers and air _____
  _____. (also / fresheners / cause / can / headaches)

- Some people get them _____, or
  because they are allergic to certain foods.
  (need / bodies / because / caffeine / their)

A 学生が授業中に居眠りをしてしまう原因と、授業中に居眠りをすることで起こりうる結果を考えましょう。まず、ヒントを参考にしながら、下の表の空欄を埋めましょう。

Causes and Effects of Sleeping in Class

Causes	Effects
1. not enough sleep	1. make the teacher angry
2. classes are not interesting or fun	2. can't …
3. little motivation to learn	3.

Hint 1

anger the teacher

Hint 2

ask questions

Hint 3

do group work

Hint 4

fail the final test

B **A** の表を参考にしながら、囲みの中の語句を使って、学生が授業中に居眠りをしてしまう原因について述べたパラグラフを完成させましょう。

> as a result　　because　　due to　　interest　　motivated　　reasons

One of the main ¹(　　　　　) some students fall asleep in class is ²(　　　　　) they don't get enough sleep at night. Another big reason is ³(　　　　　) a lack of ⁴(　　　　　) in their classes. Lastly, some students aren't ⁵(　　　　　) to do well in school. ⁶(　　　　　), they sleep during class.

C **A** で考えたことをもとに、授業中の居眠りが原因で起こりうる結果について 1 つのパラグラフを書いてみましょう。

Sleeping in class can have several consequences. First, students who fall asleep in class might _____. Second, _____. Finally, _____

_____.

11

This Is the Same, but That's Not

ハロウィーン（ハロウィン）は、欧米、特にアメリカではずっと昔から民間行事として定着していますが、日本でも最近では特に若者たちの間で人気のイベントになっています。日本でハロウィーンはどのようにして広まったのでしょうか。この Unit では、日米のハロウィーン文化の違いについて概観し、英語で比較・対照を表現するための方法を学びましょう。

Warm-Up Questions

次の質問に対して **1.** は英単語または絵を記入し、**2.** は英語で答えましょう。

1. What images come to mind when you think of Halloween? Write words or draw pictures in the bubbles.

2. Imagine you are at a Halloween costume party. Who or what are you?

➡ I'm _____.

22
Audio

How Halloween Took Off in Japan

Halloween started to become popular in Japan in the late 1990s. On October 31, 1997, Tokyo Disneyland (TDL) held its first
5▶ Halloween event called "Disney Happy Halloween." It included a 400-guest parade and special treats for kids under 12. Every year since 2000, TDL has held
10▶ its "Disney Halloween Parade."
Universal Studios Japan (USJ) opened in 2001, and began hosting its own Halloween activities a year later. The Halloween events of these two theme parks have attracted much attention and have become more exciting every year. They've helped make Halloween in Japan one of the biggest and most fun-filled celebrations of the year.

Notes fun-filled 楽しさ満載の   celebration 祭典、祝典

Comprehension Questions

本文の内容に合うように、(   ) の中から適切なものを選びましょう。

1. Tokyo Disneyland held its first Halloween event in (a. 1990   b. 1997   c. 2000).

2. During the "Disney Happy Halloween" event, (a. all visitors   b. 400 visitors   c. children under the age of 12) received special treats.

3. USJ hosted its first Halloween events in (a. 2000   b. 2001   c. 2002).

Grammar Points

(• 比較級と最上級)

形容詞と副詞の比較級・最上級には、原級に -er/-est をつけるものと more/most をつけるものがあります。good/well (better—best)，bad/badly (worse—worst)，many/much (more—most) などは不規則な変化をします。

比較級・最上級の作り方	原級	比較級	最上級
① -e で終わる語	nice	nicer	(the) nicest
→ -r, -st をつける	late	later	(the) latest
② 子音字＋y で終わる語	happy	happier	(the) happiest
→ y を i に変えて -er, -est をつける	early	earlier	(the) earliest
③ 短母音＋子音字で終わる形容詞	big	bigger	(the) biggest
→ 子音字を重ねて -er, -est をつける	hot	hotter	(the) hottest
④ 形容詞 +ly で終わる副詞	quickly	more quickly	(the) most quickly
→ more, most をつける	quietly	more quietly	(the) most quietly
⑤ 上記①〜④以外の短い語	tall	taller	(the) tallest
→ -er, -est をつける	hard	harder	(the) hardest
⑥ 上記①〜④以外の長い語	beautiful	more beautiful	(the) most beautiful
→ more, most をつける	difficult	more difficult	(the) most difficult

Grammar Practice

(   ) の中から最も適切な語句を選び、○で囲みましょう。

1. Your suitcase is (heavier / more heavy) than mine.

2. He is the (fastest / most fast) runner on the team.

3. The situation is (worse / more worse) than before.

4. This is (more / the most) interesting book I've ever read.

5. The United States produces more oil (of all / than any other) country.

6. This computer is (much better / more better) than that one.

23
Audio

Halloween in the United States and Japan

1   In the United States, Halloween is one of the most
popular events of the year, especially for children. On the evening of October 31,
neighborhoods suddenly become filled with little ghosts, vampires, princesses and
superheroes ringing doorbells and trick-or-treating. Many families display jack-o'-
5▸ lanterns with scary faces in their windows. Some schools hold Halloween dances,
while many young adults attend costume parties. On Halloween night, parents and
grandparents busily hand out treats to their "night visitors."

2   Compared to Americans, there are a few differences in the way the Japanese
celebrate Halloween. Halloween in Japan is more focused on older teens and young
10▸ adults than it is on children. Japanese children normally don't go trick-or-treating.
Halloween isn't about ghosts and haunted houses, either. It's more a celebration of
Japan's pop culture. And for thousands of university students and young working
people, that means dressing up in cosplay costumes and partying the night away.

Notes	neighborhood 近所 vampire 吸血鬼 jack-o'-lantern ジャック・オー・ランタン（カボチャちょうちん） party the night away パーティーをして夜を明かす

Comprehension Questions

本文の内容に関して、次の質問の答えとして適切なものを選びましょう。

1. What do many American families put in their windows on Halloween night?

   a. ghosts   b. candy   c. jack-o'-lanterns

2. Who is Halloween focused on in the United States?

   a. young children   b. junior and senior high school students   c. young adults

3. What does Halloween celebrate in Japan?

   a. scary things   b. Japanese pop culture   c. life and death

Writing Strategy

→ トピックセンテンス

トピックセンテンス（topic sentence）とは、そのパラグラフで書き手が伝えたいこと（main idea）を簡潔に総括した文で、通例パラグラフの冒頭に置かれます。トピックセンテンスを読めば、パラグラフのその後の展開が予想できます。

- Living in Tokyo has both advantages and disadvantages.
  ▷ advantages（長所）と disadvantages（短所）の具体例が提示される。

- There are three simple ways to save money.
  ▷ three simple ways（3つの簡単な方法）の詳細が提示される。

- In my view, the Japanese government should spend more money on education.
  ▷ 書き手がそのように考える理由や根拠が提示される。

Paragraph Building

（   ）内の語句を並び替えて、以下の4つの文をそれぞれ完成させましょう。さらに、完成した4つの文が1つのパラグラフになるように最も適切な順序に並べ、□に順番を記入しましょう。

Tortoises and Turtles

- Furthermore, tortoises have thick, dome-shaped shells, _____ and smoother.
  (are / turtle / thinner / shells / but)

tortoise

- First of all, tortoises are usually larger _____.
  (heavier / and / turtles / than / much)

- A third main difference is that tortoises are mostly land-based creatures, while turtles spend most _____.
  (lives / water / of / in / their)

- _____ and turtles?
  (tortoises / difference / the / what's / between)

turtle

73

A 以下の表は、Jim が２つの授業について答えたものです。

Name of Class	Marketing	Art History
Number of students	~25	~80
Level of difficulty: 1=easy ～ 5=difficult	4	3
Amount of homework: 1=very little ～ 5=a lot	5	2
My level of interest in the class: 1=not interesting ～ 5=very interesting	2	5

B A の表をもとに、囲みの中の語句を使って、Jim の書いた以下のパラグラフを完成させましょう。

easier   less   little   more   much   smaller

Two classes that I'm taking this semester are Marketing and Art History. Marketing is a ¹(   ) ²(   ) class (25) than Art History (80). In terms of difficulty, Art History is a ³(   ) ⁴(   ) than Marketing, and there's a lot ⁵(   ) homework. I think Art History is much ⁶(   ) interesting than Marketing.

C あなた自身が受講している授業を２つ取り上げ、以下の表に記入した後、下のパラグラフを完成させましょう。

Name of Class		
Number of students		
Level of difficulty: 1=easy ～ 5=difficult		
Amount of homework: 1=very little ～ 5=a lot		
My level of interest in the class: 1=not interesting ～ 5=very interesting		

Two classes that I'm taking this semester are _____ and _____.

_____

_____

I think _____.

What Do You Think?

宇宙開発は、科学的知識の向上につながるだけでなく、人工衛星を利用した様々なサービスの提供や産業の育成に役立つと考えられています。一方で、莫大な費用が必要なことやスペースデブリ（宇宙ごみ）による宇宙環境破壊、軍事利用の可能性などの問題も指摘されています。この Unit では、宇宙開発に関する文章を読み、英語で自分の意見を表現する方法を学びましょう。

Warm-Up Questions

次の質問に対して **1.** と **2.** は該当する答えに ☑ をつけ、**3.** は英語で答えましょう。

1. Who was the first person in space?

☐ an American   ☐ a German   ☐ a Russian

2. Who was the first person to walk on the Moon?

☐ Buzz Aldrin   ☐ Neil Armstrong   ☐ Yuri Gagarin

3. Would you like to travel to space someday?

Yes / No …because _____.

24
Audio

Space Tourism

Do you think space tourism will become popular one day? According to a well-known research center in the United States, 50% of U.S. adults believe that people will regularly travel to space as tourists in the next 50 years. However, 58% of American adults say they aren't going to take trips themselves. They think that it will be too expensive or scary, or that their age or health won't allow them to travel safely. The most common reason among people who would like to space travel is their desire to experience something unique.

Comprehension Questions

本文の内容に合うように、（　）の中から適切な語句を選びましょう。

1. (a. Less than half　b. Half　c. More than half) of U.S. adults think that space tourism will be popular in the next 50 years.

2. A majority of Americans say they (a. are going to　b. aren't going to c. might) travel to space themselves.

3. Some people won't travel to space because (a. they don't like to be in closed spaces　b. there is a long training period　c. they won't be healthy enough to travel safely).

Grammar Points

be going to と will

< be going to +動詞の原形>と<助動詞 will +動詞の原形>はいずれも未来の事柄を表しますが、ニュアンスが少し異なるので注意しましょう。

	be going to	will
肯定文	A: What are your plans for tomorrow? B: I'm going to visit my uncle. Look! That car is going to hit the bus.	A: It's really hot in here. B: I'll open the window. I wonder if she'll recognize me.
否定文	That's not going to happen.	Don't ask Mary for help. She won't say yes. *won't = will not
疑問文	Are you going to study abroad?	Will you close the door, please?

① 通例、すでに決められた事柄や前もって計画されていた事柄には be going to を用い、その場で決めた事柄については will を用います。② 現在の様子・兆候から近い将来起こると想定できる事柄やすでに計画されている未来の事柄については be going to が好まれ、明確な証拠がない場合や話者自身の考えを表す場合は will が好まれます。③ 聞き手の意志を尋ねる Will you ～? は依頼や命令の意味合いが出ることもあります。

Grammar Practice

( ) の中から最も適切な語句を選び、○で囲みましょう。

1. I know who is (going to / will) win.

2. I (am going to / will) not do it again.

3. (Are / Will) you please turn off your cell phone?

4. Look at the dark clouds. (It's going to / It'll) rain pretty soon.

5. Laura (is going to / will) have a baby in a few weeks.

6. "Someone is at the door." "(I'm going to / I'll) get it."

25 Audio

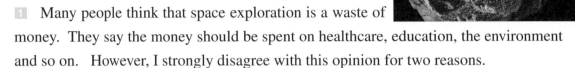

The Necessity of Space Exploration

1 Many people think that space exploration is a waste of money. They say the money should be spent on healthcare, education, the environment and so on.   However, I strongly disagree with this opinion for two reasons.

2 First, space research has led to the development of many technologies that
5▶ positively impact our daily lives, including GPS (Global Positioning System), weather forecasting and satellite television. And right now, scientists are doing medical research in space that is impossible to do on Earth—research that may save your life one day. Second, scientists agree that, for our survival, humans will eventually have to leave Earth. Therefore, we must learn how to survive for long periods of time in space
10▶ and how to live on other planets.

3 In conclusion, I believe that space exploration is necessary in order to develop new technologies and gain knowledge that will help us both now and in the future.

Notes space exploration 宇宙開発   weather forecasting 天気予報   satellite 衛星   eventually ゆくゆくは

Comprehension Questions

本文の内容に関して、次の質問の答えとして適切なものを選びましょう。

1. What is the author's opinion about space exploration?

   a. It's a waste of money.   b. It's important for our lives and future.
   c. It isn't necessary right now.

2. In what area of technology has space research helped us?

   a. business   b. communication   c. education

3. Which statement do scientists agree with?

   a. We cannot live on Earth forever.   b. We will eventually stop exploring space.
   c. We will never be able to survive in space for long periods of time.

Writing Strategy

支持文と結語文

支持文（supporting sentence）とは、トピックセンテンスの内容の理由や根拠、具体例や詳細を提示する文のことです。**結語文**（concluding sentence）とは、パラグラフの内容のまとめや結論を提示したり、トピックセンテンスで述べた主張を再度述べたりする文で、通例、パラグラフの最後に置かれます。結語文のないパラグラフもあります。

トピックセンテンス

I prefer living in a big city to living in a small town.   **支持文 1**

One reason is that big cities have a wide selection of shopping and entertainment options.   **支持文 2**

Another reason is that big cities tend to offer more career opportunities and higher salaries.   **結語文**

For these reasons, I think that big city living is more desirable than small town living.

Paragraph Building

(   ) 内の語句を並び替えて、以下の 4 つの文をそれぞれ完成させましょう。さらに、完成した 4 つの文が 1 つのパラグラフになるように最も適切な順序に並べ、□ に順番を記入しましょう。

Give Your English a Boost

□ • For these reasons, _____ an English-speaking family abroad will make you a better English speaker. (that / I / with / living / believe)

□ • One reason is _____ in English and, therefore, learn many new words and expressions. (you / be / will / immersed / because)

□ • A second reason is that it will give you _____ _____. (speak / to / confidence / English / greater)

□ • In my opinion, the best way _____ is by doing a homestay in an English-speaking country. (English / improve / skills / to / your)   **Notes**   immersed 浸って、没入して

A 以下は映画 *Back to the Future* の紹介です。あらすじとレビューに特に注目しながら読んでみましょう。

Name of movie	Back to the Future
Year of release	1985
Director	Robert Zemeckis
Main actors	Michael J. Fox, Christopher Lloyd
Genre	Science Fiction/Comedy

Story Summary　Marty McFly accidentally travels back in time from 1985 to 1955 in a time machine invented by his friend Dr. Emmett (Doc) Brown. Marty must make sure his parents meet and fall in love—so he can get back to the future.

Movie Review　In my opinion, *Back to the Future* is one of the greatest movies for three main reasons. First, the story is interesting, funny and unique. Second, the acting is excellent. Marty and Doc are a perfect match and their friendship is special. Lastly, the movie is exciting from beginning to end. There is never a dull moment.

B **A** を参考にして、あなたの好きな映画をひとつ紹介してみましょう。

Name of movie	
Year of release	
Director	
Main actors	
Genre*	
Story Summary	

Movie Review　In my opinion, _____ is

for three main reasons. First,

Second,

Finally,

*animation / action / horror / romance / drama / thriller / non-fiction / adventure / mystery

Weighing Strengths and Weaknesses

テレワークとは、情報通信技術を活用した、働く時間や場所にとらわれない柔軟な働き方の一つで、近年多くの企業で導入されています。テレワークは、仕事の効率化や働き方の多様性を支える新しい勤労形態として注目されていますが、その短所も指摘されています。この Unit では、テレワークの長所と短所について考えながら、ものごとの是非や賛否を英語で論じる方法を学びましょう。

Warm-Up Questions

次の質問に対してそれぞれ英語で答えましょう。

1. What is one good point and one bad point about telework?

Good point: _____

Bad point: _____

2. Name six jobs where telework is NOT possible.

- _____
- _____
- _____
- _____
- _____
- _____

26
Audio

Telework

Telework in Japan started in the mid-1980s when land prices in large cities were quickly rising. Workers, mainly salespersons, were sent from head
5► offices to branch offices that were closer to their homes. However, because Internet services were not widely available at that time, telework was done on a small scale. Today, thanks to smartphones and other advanced technology, telework has become a more realistic work option. Recently, the Japanese government has promoted telework as a way to modernize Japan's work system. And as many young workers look for jobs
10► that offer remote work, more and more companies are shifting to telework systems.

Notes   head office 本社   branch office 支店、支社   small scale 小規模

Comprehension Questions

本文の内容に合うように、(　　　) の中から適切な語句を選びましょう。

1. The first teleworkers in Japan worked at (a. home   b. local offices   c. main offices).

2. (a. A law   b. The economy   c. Technology) has made telework a realistic work choice.

3. Telework is a way for the government to (a. modernize   b. build   c. manage) Japan's work system.

Grammar Points

従位接続詞

文の中心となる主要な節を主節、主節に付属的な意味を追加する節を従位節といいます。従位節を導く接続詞の多くは、① 主節の内容との時間的な前後関係や同時性を表すもの、② 主節の内容の原因・理由を表すもの、③ 主節の内容と従位節の内容が逆接的・対照的であることを表すもの、④ 主節の内容が成立するための条件を表すもの、に分類できます。

主節との意味関係	接続詞	例文
①時間関係	before, after, when, as など	• I left the office before the fire alarm went off. • After I left the office, the fire alarm went off.
②因果関係	because, since, as など	• They canceled the festival because it was raining. • Since it was raining, they canceled the festival.
③逆接・対比関係	although, while, whereas など	• Although Brian is rich, he is not happy at all. • Some people prefer living alone, while others don't.
④条件	if, unless, in case など	• If you study hard, you'll get a good job. • You won't get a good job unless you study hard.

Grammar Practice

(　) の中から最も適切な語句を選び、○で囲みましょう。

1. I looked for a pay phone (because / so) my cell phone wasn't working.

2. (Since / Although) the traffic was extremely bad, we arrived there on time.

3. You should go home (before / until) it gets dark.

4. Hurry up! You'll miss the train (if / unless) you leave now.

5. We visited many museums (while / during) we were in Paris.

6. We'll provide more information (once / unless) it becomes available.

27
Audio

Is Telework Good or Bad for Workers and Their Companies?

■ When it comes to telework in Japan, there are several pros and cons to think about. On the plus side, workers don't have to ride crowded trains every day, which is a stressful time for many people. They have more time to help out around the house, be with their families and enjoy hobbies. Companies save money on office space and other costs such as transportation for workers.

■ On the other hand, it's difficult for teleworkers to keep personal connections with their co-workers since online meetings focus on business. Some teleworkers say they get less exercise. Others find it difficult to work at home when they have small children. And although most teleworkers work better at home than at the office, many office managers worry that the opposite is true.

■ In summary, the question of whether telework is good or bad really depends on the situation of the workers and the companies they work for.

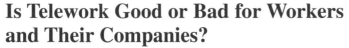

Notes　pros and cons 賛否、良し悪し　transportation 交通費　co-worker 同僚　opposite 反対、逆

Comprehension Questions

本文の内容に関して、次の質問の答えとして適切なものを選びましょう。

1. What does telework allow workers to do?

　a. eat healthier food　　b. enjoy more family time　c. meet friends more often

2. What do companies with a telework system save money on?

　a. office space　　　　b. worker salaries　　　c. bonus payments

3. What is generally true about teleworkers?

　a. They work better at the office.　　b. They work better at home.
　c. They perform the same quality of work at home as they do at the office.

Writing Strategy

(→ 対比や対照を表す)

(1) 接続詞として働くもの
   < while, whereas など >

   - His computer is new, while mine is quite old.

(2) 前置詞として働くもの
   < unlike, in contrast to, as opposed to など >

   - Unlike his computer, mine is quite old.

(3) 副詞語句として働くもの
   < in contrast, on the other hand など >

   - His computer is new. In contrast, mine is quite old.

Paragraph Building

(　　) 内の語句を並び替えて、以下の 4 つの文をそれぞれ完成させましょう。さらに、完成した 4 つの文が 1 つのパラグラフになるように最も適切な順序に並べ、□ に順番を記入しましょう。

Hostel Considerations

□ • On the other hand, unless ＿＿＿＿＿＿＿＿＿＿＿＿＿＿, a hostel won't allow you much privacy. (a / room / you / single / get)

□ • Hostels are also a good choice ＿＿＿＿＿＿＿＿＿＿＿＿＿＿ from different countries. (meeting / like / you / if / people)

□ • And there's always the risk of theft when ＿＿＿＿＿＿＿＿＿＿＿＿ ＿＿＿＿＿. (strangers / share / with / you / a room)

□ • Hostels are popular among young travelers, mainly ＿＿＿＿＿＿＿＿＿ ＿＿＿＿＿＿＿＿＿＿＿. (hotels / cheaper / because / than / they're)

Notes　theft 盗難

A 大学教育に関して良いと思うことと良くないと思うことを考えましょう。ヒントを参考に、良くないと思う点を 3 つ考え、下の表に記入しましょう。

Pros and Cons of a University Education

Pros		Cons	
1.	Gain knowledge and skills	1.	Classes, books, etc. are expensive
2.	Make new friends and connections	2.	
3.	Earn more money	3.	
4.	Higher possibility of promotion	4.	

Ideas:

| expensive | homework | tests | boring classes |

B A の表を参考にしながら、囲みの中の語句を使って、大学教育の良い点について述べたパラグラフを完成させましょう。

> advantages   graduate   high school   learn   moving up   salary

Let me explain four ¹(   ) of a university education. First, you gain knowledge and ²(   ) new skills. Second, you make new friends and connections that may help you after you ³(   ). Third, when you start working, your ⁴(   ) will probably be higher than that of a ⁵(   ) graduate. And fourth, you'll have a better chance of ⁶(   ) in your company.

C A で考えたことをもとに、B に続くパラグラフを書いてみましょう。

On the other hand, attending university has its disadvantages, too. First, classes, books, etc. are expensive. Second, _____.

Third, _____.

And lastly, _____.

14

One Step at a Time

私たちは日常の中で様々な商品やサービスを購入して生活しています。しかし、自分が購入した商品やサービスについて、どのような心理的過程を経て購入の決定に至ったのかをわざわざ考えたり、分析したりすることは通常ありません。この Unit では、消費者の購買意思決定過程を説明した文章を読み、ものごとの過程や手順を説明するのに役立つ英語表現を学びましょう。

次の質問に対して **1.** は重要度の高い順に数字を記入し、**2.** は該当する答えに ☑ をつけ、**3.** は英語で答えましょう。

1. From 1 (most important) to 5 (least important), what do you think about when you shop for clothes?

   _____ brand　　_____ color　　_____ design/style　　_____ price　　_____ quality

2. How often do you shop online?

   ☐ quite often　　☐ often　　☐ sometimes　　☐ not very often　　☐ never

3. What are two things that you have bought recently? _____ /_____

**28
Audio**

Buying Shortcuts

Sometimes people don't have the time or desire to think carefully about everything they buy. Instead, rules of thumb
5▸ are used to make their buying decisions easier. One rule of thumb is "Buy the cheapest one."
These people think only about where the item is sold at the lowest price. A second rule of thumb is "You get what you pay for." These consumers are attracted by quality.
10▸ They believe that higher price means higher quality. A third rule of thumb is "Buy the same thing you always do." This is known as brand loyalty. These consumers trust the brand and see no reason to try anything else.

Notes shortcut 近道　rule of thumb 大まかな方法、経験則　consumer 消費者　brand loyalty ブランド信仰

Comprehension Questions

本文の内容に合うように、（　）の中から適切な語句を選びましょう。

1. Sometimes people use rules of thumb to (a. save time   b. find the best product at the cheapest price   c. make careful decisions).

2. A person who buys (a. the cheapest   b. the most expensive   c. the most attractive) item is following the "You get what you pay for" rule of thumb.

3. People who use the "Buy the same thing you always do" rule of thumb (a. change brands for no reason   b. believe in the brand   c. like to try different brands).

Grammar Points

受動態

動作の対象を主語にして「(人・物が)～される」という意味を表す文を受動態といい、< be 動詞＋過去分詞 >の形で表します。動作主は< by ＋動作主 >で表しますが、省略されることもよくあります。

| 能動態： | All his colleagues | respect | him. |

| 受動態： | He | is respected | by all his colleagues. |

(1) 受動態の否定文・疑問文

- The letter was not written by John.
- Was the letter written by John?

(2) 助動詞・進行形・完了時制を含む文の受動態

- The software can be downloaded here.
- The wall is being painted by them.
- The same error has been reported by many users.

Grammar Practice

(   )の中から最も適切な語句を選び、○で囲みましょう。

1. English is (speaking / spoken) in many countries.

2. Her wallet was (looked / found) by the police.

3. The university was (found / founded) in 1890.

4. (Did / Were) these books written by the same author?

5. All tickets (must be reserved / must have reserved) in advance.

6. The meeting room (is being used / is been using) now.

29
Audio

How Buying Decisions Are Made

[1]   The decision to buy a product may take only a few seconds, or it could take days, weeks, months, or even years. Although the time required to buy a product varies, people usually go through a four-stage process before buying most things.

[2]   **Stage 1: Understanding the Need** Stage one is recognizing the need for the
5▶ product.

[3]   **Stage 2: Information Gathering** In the second stage, information about the product is collected. This is done by searching the Internet, asking friends, talking to sales assistants, etc.

[4]   **Stage 3: Evaluating Options & Purchase** In this stage, the available choices are
10▶ compared and evaluated—things like price, design, quality, color and brand. The desired product is then chosen and purchased.

[5]   **Stage 4: After-Purchase Evaluation** In the final stage, the product is used and evaluated. A positive evaluation means there is a good chance that the product will be purchased again the next time it is needed.

Notes   vary 変わる、異なる   recognize 認識する   evaluate 評価する   compare 比較する

Comprehension Questions

本文の内容に関して、次の質問の答えとして適切なものを選びましょう。

1. How long does it usually take a person to make a buying decision?

a. a few seconds   b. several minutes   c. case by case

2. In which stage might a consumer ask friends for information about a product?

a. Stage 2   b. Stage 3   c. Stage 4

3. What does the consumer do in Stage 4?

a. decide which product to buy   b. purchase the product   c. use the product

Writing Strategy

(• 出来事の前後関係を表す)

(1) 時間の前後関係を表す接続詞

< before, after, as soon as, by the time など >

- I finished my homework before I went to bed.

   先の出来事 　　　　　　　　　後の出来事

(2) 時間の前後関係を表す前置詞

< before, after, by, until など >

- I went to bed after finishing my homework.

   後の出来事 　　　　　　　　先の出来事

(3) 順序を表す副詞語句

< first, second, next, then, finally など >

- First, I took an exam. Then I had an interview the following week.

   先の出来事 　　　　　　　　　　　後の出来事

Paragraph Building

(　　) 内の語句を並び替えて、下の 4 つの文をそれぞれ完成させましょう。さらに、1 つのパラグラフができるように、完成した 4 つの文を最も適切な順序に並べ、□に番号を記入しましょう。

Getting Things Done

□ • Next, _____ to do those things, and stick to your plan! (the / schedule / times / day / during)

□ • In order to make your day more productive, start by listing 3 or 4 _____ _____ in order of importance. (you / do / things / to / need)

□ • _____, review what worked and what didn't work, and make any necessary adjustments. (the day / end / at / the / of)

□ • Then, before you begin your work, put your phone on silent mode, and _____ _____. (quiet / a / place / to / move)

Notes   stick to ~ ~を固く守る   productive 生産的な   adjustment 調整

91

A 以下はインスタントラーメンの作り方の手順を示したものです。正しい順序になるように、□に1〜6の番号を記入しましょう。

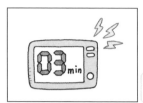

B 囲みの中の語句を使って、インスタントラーメンの作り方を説明してみましょう。

enjoy your meal	open the lid	pour boiling water
stir the noodles well	wait 3 minutes	weigh down the lid

How to Make Instant Noodles

First, ¹( ) halfway. Next, ²( ) to the fill line on the inside of the container. After that, ³( ) with chopsticks or a small plate. Then ⁴( ). Finally, ⁵( ) with chopsticks. ⁶( )!

C インスタントラーメン以外のものを1つ取り上げ、簡単なレシピを書いてみましょう。下のヒントも参考にしてみてください。

How to Make _____

First, _____

_____

_____

Finally, _____

Ideas: instant coffee, hot cocoa, scrambled eggs, French toast

92

15

Data Presentation the Simple Way

グラフは数値の変化、大小関係、割合などの情報を視覚的に表したもので、プレゼンテーションなどによく用いられます。グラフにはいろいろな種類があり、提示するデータの種類や伝えたいデータの特徴によって、使うべきグラフも異なります。この Unit では、代表的なグラフを例にとり、視覚的に提示されたデータを英語で的確に説明するための練習をしましょう。

Warm-Up Questions

次の質問に対してそれぞれ英語で答えましょう。**3.** と **5.** は該当する答えに☑️をつけ、**5.** では使用したものについても答えましょう。

1. What was your last presentation about? _____

2. When did you make it? _____

3. Was it a solo presentation or a group presentation?　　□Solo　　□Group

4. How long was your presentation? _____ minutes

5. Did you use visual tools such as photographs, illustrations, videos or graphs?

　　□ Yes, I used _____.　　□No, I didn't.

30 Audio

Graphs

Graphs, or charts, are a useful tool for anyone who has to make a presentation. They're easy to understand and attract the attention of the audience. Three of the most common types of graphs are pie graphs, bar graphs and line graphs. Pie graphs, or circle graphs, display how a whole thing is divided into different parts, or "slices." Bar graphs show amounts as bars of different lengths. Line graphs track changes that happen over periods of time. When smaller changes occur over longer time periods, line graphs are preferable to bar graphs. Graphs often include color or shading, which allows readers to understand the information more easily.

Notes audience 聴衆　amount 分量

Comprehension Questions

本文の内容に合うように、(　　) の中から適切な語句を選びましょう。

1. Another word for "graph" is (a. chart　b. data　c. slide).

2. A (a. round graph　b. slice graph　c. circle graph) is the same as a pie graph.

3. A (a. bar graph　b. line graph　c. pie graph) is best for showing small changes over a long period of time.

Grammar Points

→ 関係代名詞

関係代名詞が導く節は、前の名詞（先行詞）をより詳しく説明する働きをします。関係代名詞が節の中で担う役割によって、主格、目的格、所有格の３つに分けられます。目的格の関係代名詞はしばしば省略されます。who, whom, which は、先行詞が人を表すか物（人以外）を表すかによって使い分ける必要があるので注意しましょう。

関係代名詞	先行詞	格	例文
who	人	主格	Jason has a brother who is a dentist. The man who lives next door is Jason's brother.
whom*	人	目的格	I know the professor whom he met yesterday. The person whom I admire most is my father.
which**	物	主格	He has an old car which often breaks down.
		目的格	The museum which we visited last year is now closed.
that	人 / 物	主格	The police officer that spoke to me had a strong accent.
		目的格	The police officer that I spoke to had a strong accent.
whose	人 / 物	所有格	That's the boy whose father is a famous comedian. The house whose roof you can see is my cousin's.

* whom はしばしば省略されます。また、略式では who を whom の代わりに用いることもあります。
** 多くの場合、which よりも that を用いる方が一般的です。

Grammar Practice

(   ) の中から最も適切な語句を選び、○で囲みましょう。

1. That is the student (who / whom) asked for help.

2. The man (that / which) I talked to yesterday was very friendly.

3. That was one of the songs (which inspired me / which I was inspired).

4. There were several people (that / whose) names I could not remember.

5. I have a friend (who has a son / whose son) works for ABC Company.

6. One of the countries that I want to (visit / go there) is Australia.

31 Audio

Graph Talk

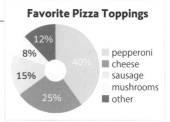

Favorite Pizza Toppings

pepperoni
cheese
sausage
mushrooms
other

1 This is a graph of the favorite toppings of pizza eaters. Pepperoni is the favorite topping of 40% of pizza eaters. Next comes cheese (25%), followed by sausage (15%) and mushrooms (8%). Various other items are the favorite toppings of 12% of pizza eaters.

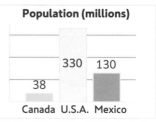

Population (millions)

Canada   U.S.A.   Mexico

2 This is a graph showing the number of people who live in the U.S.A., Canada and Mexico. As you can see, the U.S.A. has the largest population, with 330 million people. Mexico has 130 million people, and Canada 38 million.

3 This graph shows the number of minicars sold in Japan between 2011 and 2018. In 2011, 1.52 million cars were sold. Sales rose sharply over the next three years, and peaked at 2.27 million units in 2014. Purchases fell to 1.90 million units in 2015 and 1.73 million units in 2016. They then increased steadily, reaching 1.92 million units in 2018.

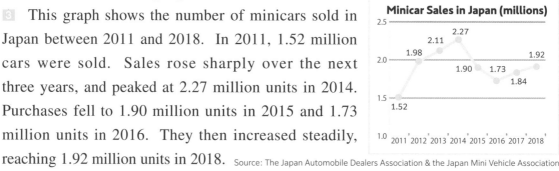

Source: The Japan Automobile Dealers Association & the Japan Mini Vehicle Association

Comprehension Questions

本文の内容に関して、次の質問の答えとして適切なものを選びましょう。

1. Graph 1: What is the favorite topping of one-quarter of pizza eaters?

   a. cheese   b. pepperoni   c. mushrooms

2. Graph 2: What is the combined population of the three countries?

   a. about 50 million   b. about 500 million   c. about 5 billion

3. Graph 3: How many minicars were sold in Japan during the years 2011-2014?

   a. about 3 million   b. about 6 million   c. about 8 million

Writing Strategy

数値の動向を表す

数値の増減を表す	名詞	動詞
名 増加 / 動 増加する	an increase / a rise / a climb	increase / rise / climb
名 減少 / 動 減少する	a decrease / a fall / a drop	decrease / fall / drop

変化の程度を表す	形容詞	副詞
形 かなりの / 副 かなり	considerable / significant	considerably / significantly
形 急な / 副 急に	rapid / sharp	rapidly / sharply
形 漸進的な / 副 徐々に	gradual	gradually
形 わずかな / 副 わずかに	slight	slightly

例 Sales dropped sharply in 2020. = In 2020 there was a sharp drop in sales.

Paragraph Building

（　　）内の語句を並び替えて、以下の 4 つの文をそれぞれ完成させましょう。さらに、完成した 4 つの文が 1 つのパラグラフになるように最も適切な順序に並べ、□に順番を記入しましょう。

Blood Type Distribution in Japan

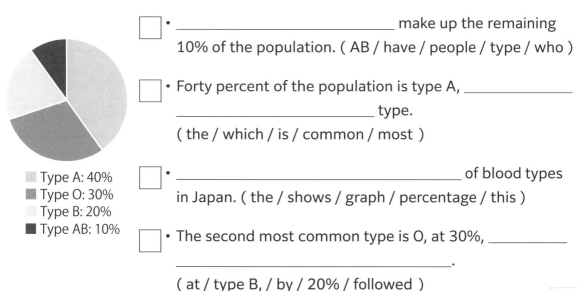

□ • _____ make up the remaining 10% of the population. (AB / have / people / type / who)

□ • Forty percent of the population is type A, _____ _____ type.
(the / which / is / common / most)

□ • _____ of blood types in Japan. (the / shows / graph / percentage / this)

□ • The second most common type is O, at 30%, _____ _____.
(at / type B, / by / 20% / followed)

Type A: 40%
Type O: 30%
Type B: 20%
Type AB: 10%

A 以下の表は Mike がサイクリングで走った曜日ごとの走行距離を表しています。水曜日以降の数値を右のグラフに記入して、線グラフを完成させましょう。

Day	Number of kilometers
Monday	50
Tuesday	20
Wednesday	60
Thursday	60
Friday	65
Saturday	90
Sunday	85

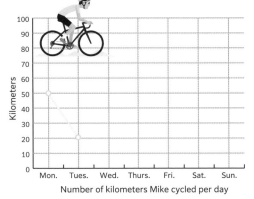

Number of kilometers Mike cycled per day

B 囲みの中の語句を使って、**A** のグラフの説明を完成させましょう。

> decreased considerably increased significantly
> sharp climb slightly less slight rise

Mike cycled 50 km on Monday. On Tuesday, the distance that he covered
¹( ) to just 20 km. However, it ²( ) to
60 km on both Wednesday and Thursday. There was a ³( )
to 65 km on Friday, and a ⁴( ) to 90 km on Saturday. He
covered 85 kilometers on Sunday, which was ⁵( ) than the
previous day.

C **A**、**B** で学んだことを参考にして、下のグラフを自分の言葉で説明してみましょう。

This graph shows _____ from October 2019 to March 2020.

It rained _____ mm in October 2019. Rainfall _____ sharply in

November to _____ mm. _____

_____

_____

_____

_____

_____

Rainfall in ABC City from October 2019 to March 2020 (mm)

180
90
50
45
60
105

Oct. Nov. Dec. Jan. Feb. Mar.

付録

状態動詞の種類 (Unit 1, Unit 5)

状態動詞の種類	例文
①通例進行形にならないもの (know, want, need, seem, own, belong など)	Kate seems happy. ✗ Kate is seeming happy.
②状態と動作・活動の両方の意味を持つもの ※進行形の場合、(意図的な) 動作・活動を表す (look, have, taste, smell, think など)	The cake looks delicious. I'm looking at the bird over there.
③現在形と進行形が基本的に同じ意味を表すもの (feel, hurt, ache, itch など)	I feel sick. I'm feeling sick.

代表的な自動詞と他動詞 (Unit 2)

自動詞 (目的語をとらない)	他動詞 (目的語をとる)
appear, arrive, be, come, cry, die, disappear, fall, go, happen, laugh, lie, live, occur, remain, rise, seem, sit, sleep, smile, stay, talk	accompany, approach, attend, consider, contact, discuss, enjoy, enter, follow, have, lay, like, love, marry, obey, own, raise, reach, resemble

代表的な不可算名詞 (Unit 3)

飲食物	beef, bread, butter, cheese, coffee, juice, milk, rice, salt, soup, sugar, tea, water, wine
物質・素材	cotton, glass, gold, iron, metal, oil, plastic, silk, silver, steel, wood
気象・自然現象	fog, heat, ice, lightning, rain, snow, weather, wind
抽象名詞	advice, existence, freedom, fun, harm, help, information, love, luck, progress, respect, time, violence, wisdom
その他	baggage, equipment, furniture, homework, luggage, money, vocabulary

to 不定詞・動名詞を目的語にとる動詞 (Unit 9)

to 不定詞だけを目的語にとる動詞

afford, attempt, decide, desire, determine, expect, hope, learn, manage, offer, pretend, promise, refuse, want, wish

動名詞だけを目的語にとる動詞

admit, avoid, consider, deny, enjoy, finish, give up, imagine, mind, postpone, put off, quit, stop*, suggest

*stop to smoke「タバコを吸うために立ち止まる」のような場合の stop は自動詞で、to 不定詞を目的語にとっているわけではないことに注意。(cf. stop smoking「タバコを吸うのをやめる」)

to 不定詞と動名詞のいずれも目的語にとる動詞

begin, continue, forget*, hate, like, love, prefer, regret*, remember*, start, try*

*to 不定詞と動名詞のどちらを目的語にとるかによって意味が異なるものに注意。
  forget to do「～することを忘れる」/ forget doing「～したことを忘れる」
  regret to do「残念ながら～する」/ regret doing「～したことを後悔する」
  remember to do「忘れずに～する」/ remember doing「～したことを覚えている」
  try to do「～しようと試みる」/ try doing「試しに～してみる」

不規則な変化をする比較級・最上級 (Unit 11)

原級	比較級	最上級
good/well	better	(the) best
bad/badly	worse	(the) worst
many/much	more	(the) most
little	less	(the) least
far	further [farther]	(the) furthest [farthest]

代表的な従位接続詞 (Unit 13)

時間	before after when while	• We arrived at the hotel before it started raining. • After we arrived at the hotel, it started raining. • Please don't forget to call me when you get home. • We visited many museums while we stayed in Paris.
原因・理由	because since as	• I didn't have time to eat lunch because I was very busy. • Since I was very busy, I didn't have time to eat lunch. • As I was very busy, I didn't have time to eat lunch.
逆接・対比	although while whereas	• Although he is old, he is still active as a researcher. • Some people like baseball, while others like basketball. • Some people like baseball, whereas others like basketball.
条件	if unless in case	• If she speaks slowly, I can understand her English. • I can't understand her English unless she speaks slowly. • You should insure your house in case there's a fire.

受動態と時制 (Unit 14)

現在時制	The doctor examines the patient.	The patient is examined by the doctor.
過去時制	The doctor examined the patient.	The patient was examined by the doctor.
will（未来）	The doctor will examine the patient.	The patient will be examined by the doctor.
be going to（未来）	The doctor is going to examine the patient.	The patient is going to be examined by the doctor.
現在進行形	The doctor is examining the patient.	The patient is being examined by the doctor.
過去進行形	The doctor was examining the patient.	The patient was being examined by the doctor.
現在完了形	The doctor has examined the patient.	The patient has been examined by the doctor.

数値を表す表現

分数

※分子は基数（one, two, three ...）、分母は序数（third, fourth, fifth ...）で表す。分子が 2 以上の場合、分母の序数を複数形にする。

$\frac{1}{2}$ (one-half) $\frac{1}{3}$ (one-third) $\frac{2}{3}$ (two-thirds) $\frac{3}{4}$ (three-fourths/three-quarters)

$\frac{4}{5}$ (four-fifths) $1\frac{5}{6}$ (one and five-sixths)

小数

※小数点は point と読む。小数点以下は、数字を 1 つずつ読む。

2.5 (two point five)   0.97 (zero point nine seven)

3.705 (three point seven oh [zero] five)

長さ

30 cm (thirty centimeters)   10 m (ten meters)   7.6 km (seven point six kilometers)

面積

4 m × 6 m (four meters by six meters)

65㎡ (sixty-five square meters)   4 ha (four hectares)

温度

20 °C (twenty degrees Celsius [centigrade])

−5 °C (minus 5 degrees Celsius [centigrade])

100 °C (one hundred degrees Celsius [centigrade]) = 212 °F (two hundred twelve degrees Fahrenheit)

クラス用音声CD有り（別売）

Jigsaw INTRO — Insightful Reading to Successful Writing
パラグラフのパターン別に学んで磨く英語力〈初級編〉

2021年1月20日　初版発行
2024年4月20日　第 3 刷

著　者　Robert Hickling / 八島 純
発行者　松村達生
発行所　センゲージ ラーニング株式会社
　　　　〒102-0073　東京都千代田区九段北1-11-11　第2フナトビル5階
　　　　電話 03-3511-4392
　　　　FAX 03-3511-4391
　　　　e-mail: eltjapan@cengage.com
　　　　copyright © 2021 センゲージ ラーニング株式会社

装丁・組版　　藤原志麻（クリエイド・ラーニング株式会社）
編集協力　　　クリエイド・ラーニング株式会社
本文イラスト　大塚砂織 / 角 しんさく
印刷・製本　　株式会社エデュプレス

ISBN 978-4-86312-386-1